Cambridge Elements ≡

Elements in Philosophy and Logic
edited by
Bradley Armour-Garb
SUNY Albany
Frederick Kroon
The University of Auckland

MEINONGIANISM

Maria Elisabeth Reicher
RWTH Aachen University

CAMBRIDGE
UNIVERSITY PRESS

Shaftesbury Road, Cambridge CB2 8EA, United Kingdom

One Liberty Plaza, 20th Floor, New York, NY 10006, USA

477 Williamstown Road, Port Melbourne, VIC 3207, Australia

314–321, 3rd Floor, Plot 3, Splendor Forum, Jasola District Centre, New Delhi – 110025, India

103 Penang Road, #05–06/07, Visioncrest Commercial, Singapore 238467

Cambridge University Press is part of Cambridge University Press & Assessment, a department of the University of Cambridge.

We share the University's mission to contribute to society through the pursuit of education, learning and research at the highest international levels of excellence.

www.cambridge.org
Information on this title: www.cambridge.org/9781009507479

DOI: 10.1017/9781009181068

First published 2024

A catalogue record for this publication is available from the British Library.

ISBN 978-1-009-50747-9 Hardback
ISBN 978-1-009-18107-5 Paperback
ISSN 2516-418X (online)
ISSN 2516-4171 (print)

Cambridge University Press & Assessment has no responsibility for the persistence or accuracy of URLs for external or third-party internet websites referred to in this publication and does not guarantee that any content on such websites is, or will remain, accurate or appropriate.

Meinongianism

Elements in Philosophy and Logic

DOI: 10.1017/9781009181068
First published online: December 2024

Maria Elisabeth Reicher
RWTH Aachen University

Author for correspondence: Maria Elisabeth Reicher,
maria.reicher-marek@rwth-aachen.de

Abstract: *Meinongianism* (named after Alexius Meinong) is, roughly, the view that there are not only existent but also nonexistent objects. In this Element, Meinong's so-called object theory as well as "neo-Meinongian" reconstructions are presented and discussed, especially with respect to logical issues, both from a historical and a systematic perspective. Among others, the following topics are addressed: basic principles and motivations for Meinongianism; the distinction between "there is" ("∃x") and "exists" ("E!"); interpretations and kinds of quantification; Meinongianism, the principle of excluded middle, and the principle of non-contradiction; the nuclear–extranuclear distinction and modes of predication; varieties of neo-Meinongianism and Meinongian logics.

Keywords: Alexius Meinong, neo-Meinongianism, Meinongian logics, existence, quantification

ISBNs: 9781009507479 (HB), 9781009181075 (PB), 9781009181068 (OC)
ISSNs: 2516-418X (online), 2516-4171 (print)

Contents

1 Meinongianism: Basic Principles, Motivations, and Brief History

1.1 Basic Principles

By default, Meinongianism is roughly understood as the view that there are objects that do not exist, or, in short, that there are nonexistent objects.[1] It goes back to the Austrian philosopher Alexius Meinong (1853–1920).[2] Its basic tenet was first formulated in Meinong's famous paper "Über Gegenstandstheorie" (1904, English translation: "The Theory of Objects", 1960): "Those who like paradoxical modes of expression could very well say: 'There are objects of which it is true that there are no such objects'" (Meinong, 1904/1960: 83[3]).

Meinong, however, is quick to clarify that the "paradoxical mode of expression" is not to be taken at face value. He immediately resolves the apparent paradox as follows: The first occurrence of "there are" in "There are objects of which it is true that there are no such objects" differs in meaning from its second occurrence. The second occurrence ("there are no such objects") is close to its standard meaning in everyday language, for instance in: "There is a prime number between 3 and 7," "There is no largest natural number," "There are black swans," "There are no unicorns." "There are no such objects" means, in Meinong's own terms: "These objects do not have being of any kind." The whole principle is therefore to be read as follows: "There are objects of which it is true that these objects do not have being of any kind," or, briefly: "There are beingless objects."

For the sake of historical accuracy, it should be noted that Meinong distinguishes between two kinds of being, which he calls subsistence (*Bestand*) and existence (*Existenz*). Some kinds of objects (notably those which Meinong calls "ideal objects", for instance numbers, propositions, and properties) only subsist (*bestehen*); others (the "real objects", i.e., material and mental objects) both subsist and exist.

For the sake of simplicity, however, I will ignore this distinction and simply treat "being" and "existence" as synonyms (in accordance with most neo-Meinongians). Hence we arrive at the formulation: There are objects that do not exist, or, alternatively: There are nonexistent objects. In what follows, I shall refer to this basic Meinongian principle as "M".

So it is clear that within Meinongianism it is assumed that there is a semantic difference between "there is" and "exists". Moreover, "exists" entails "there is",

---

[1] However, there are several versions of so-called neo-Meinongianism that do not fit this characterization. Some "neo-Meinongians" interpret Meinongian objects as existent abstract objects; others take them to exist in nonactual possible (or even impossible) worlds. For the relation between Meinongianism and neo-Meinongianism, see the end of this subsection.

[2] For an excellent overview of Meinong's life and work, see Marek (2022).

[3] The reference is to the English translation.

but not the other way around: "Fs exist" implies "There are Fs"; but "There are Fs" does not imply "Fs exist." It should also be sufficiently clear what the Meinongian "exists" means: Its meaning is close (if not identical) to the standard natural language meaning of "there is" in most everyday contexts, such as in "There are white whales"; "There are prime numbers bigger than 100"; "There is an interesting exhibition in the MOMA right now." It is not yet clear, however, just what the Meinongian "there is" is supposed to mean. This is one of the notorious questions of Meinongianism.

There are, in principle, two possible explanations: Some assume that the Meinongian "there is" expresses a different kind of being, distinct from existence. Others claim that it expresses no kind of being at all, that it is – as it were – "ontologically neutral".[4] This issue is closely related to the question of how the quantifier is to be interpreted in Meinongianism (which will be discussed in Section 3).

Standard examples of nonexistent objects are the golden mountain, the round square, Pegasus (i.e., the flying horse from Greek mythology), Sherlock Holmes, the present king of France. The two most basic principles of Meinongianism can be formulated, in a slightly simplified manner, as follows:

(CP) To every set of properties, there is a corresponding object, either an existent or a nonexistent one, which has all and only the properties in the set.[5] In other words, to every description, there is a corresponding object that satisfies the description.

(IP) An object's *so-being* (*Sosein*, i.e., its characterizing properties, which belong to the set mentioned in CP) is independent of its *being* (*Sein*, i.e., its ontological status as either an existent or a nonexistent object).[6]

---

[4] Meinong himself wavers between these two interpretations. As noted, Meinong distinguishes between two kinds of being – existence and subsistence. The status of those objects that have neither of these he calls *Außersein* (approximately: *beyond being*). Until the end of his academic life, Meinong struggled with the question of whether *Außersein* is a third kind of being or whether it is ontologically neutral. It seems that he initially held the neutrality view, but gradually moved toward the kind-of-being view. We shall come back to this topic in Subsection 3.3.

[5] ... and perhaps also those properties that are logically entailed by the properties in the set. At any rate, most objects are *incompletely determined* (see Subsection 2.2), and all incompletely determined objects are nonexistent. Consequently, for instance, the object that corresponds to the description "the present prime minister of Hungary" is a nonexistent object (even if there exists a person who is the present prime minister of Hungary) because the corresponding object is neither male nor female, has no particular age, no particular size, no particular political views etc., and such an object cannot exist.

[6] In other words, an object's characterizing properties entail neither the object's existence nor the object's nonexistence. There is, however, an exception to IP: If an object's characterizing properties are contradictory, the object cannot exist. The terminology of *Sosein* and *Sein* goes back to Meinong (1904/1960).

The first of these two principles (CP) is often called the *Characterization Principle* or *Characterization Postulate*; the second (IP) is known as the *Principle of Independence.*[7] Take, for instance, the description "the blue". According to CP, there is an object corresponding to this description that has being blue as its sole property – namely, the object The Blue.[8] Similarly, there is an object corresponding to the description "the golden mountain", namely, The Golden Mountain, that is, an object that is golden and a mountain and has no further properties. There is even an object corresponding to every incoherent description; for instance, there is an object that corresponds to the description "the round square", that is, an object that is both round and a square.

It should be noted that The Blue, The Golden Mountain, The Round Square, and so on, are *objects* that *have* the properties mentioned in the respective descriptions – but they are not properties themselves.[9] It should also be clear that these objects are not mental entities. They are objective and independent of (and therefore not constitutive parts of) anybody's thoughts, imaginations, or other mental acts.

A note on terminology: As we will see, there are various versions of Meinongianism, and some of them are incompatible with others. At least two versions of Meinongianism can be found in Meinong himself (see Section 4), plus a variety of distinct "neo-Meinongian" theories (see Section 5), some of which diverge considerably from both versions of Meinong's Meinongianism. This diversity threatens to render the very concept of Meinongianism elusive. In order to avoid this consequence, I will restrict the use of the term "Meinongianism" in the following way: I classify all and only those philosophers as "Meinongians" who accept (1) principle M (and a distinction between "there is" and "exists"), (2) some version of CP (not necessarily the one previously formulated), and (3) IP.

At the same time, the term "neo-Meinongianism" is often used in the current literature, but – to my knowledge – it is nowhere explicated in terms of common principles, and its extension is not clearly delimited. It is usually used as a collective term denoting philosophers from 1950 onwards who were somehow interested in, and sympathetic to, Meinongian ideas, and who wanted to show

---

[7] These principles are mentioned, for instance, in Findlay (1963); Parsons (1980); Routley (1980); Lambert (1983); Zalta (1988); Perszyk (1993); Jacquette (1996); Priest (2005); Sendlak (2022).

[8] Following a familiar convention, I will call such entities "Meinongian objects". For the sake of convenience, I will use "title case" for the construction of names for Meinongian objects, e.g., "The Blue" is the name of the object that has being blue as its sole property; "The Blue and Round" is the name of the object that has being blue and being round as its sole properties; "The Golden Mountain" is the name of the object that has being golden and being a mountain as its sole properties.

[9] Some neo-Meinongians, however, interpret Meinongian objects as *sets of properties*. See Subsection 5.2.

that Meinongianism is consistent (or can be reconstructed so that it is) and has a number of interesting applications.

Not all of the philosophers who are usually subsumed under the heading "neo-Meinongianism" accept the principles M, CP, and IP. However, since the purpose of this Element is to introduce the reader to Meinongianism as it is usually understood in contemporary philosophy, prominent so-called neo-Meinongian theories will also be included even if they are not Meinongian in the sense characterized here. I will use the term "neo-Meinongianism" to include all contemporary philosophers who are Meinongians in the sense explained in this subsection and/or consider themselves to be Meinongians, and/or are usually classified as Meinongians in the current literature.

According to this taxonomy, some neo-Meinongians are not Meinongians (see Section 5); and there is evidence that even Meinong himself ultimately ceased to be a Meinongian (see Section 4). On the other hand, some neo-Meinongians *are* Meinongians in the explicated sense (or at least have been Meinongians during a certain period); and I will use the term "Meinongian" for them too.[10]

1.2 Motivations

1.2.1 The Problem of Intentional Directedness toward the Nonexistent

The two main motives for Meinongianism are *the problem of intentional directedness toward something that does not exist* and the *problem of negative (singular) existence statements*. The concept of intentionality has its origin in medieval philosophy, but its presence in twentieth-century and contemporary philosophy is due to Franz Brentano (1838–1917). Brentano formulated the so-called principle of intentionality: *Every mental phenomenon (be it a presentation, a judgment, or an emotion) is intentionally directed toward some object.* This "intentional directedness" is, according to Brentano, the mark of the mental, the feature that distinguishes mental from physical phenomena (Brentano, 1874).

The principle of intentionality, however, raises the following puzzle: Not all mental acts are directed toward something *existent*. One may think of, imagine, dream of, hope for, or fear something that does not exist. One may even (in the case of hallucinations) sense something that does not exist. If we accept the principle of intentionality and, at the same time, assume that the nonexistent is just nothing, we are led into outright contradiction. Consider:

---

[10] To disclose my own point of view: I am neither a Meinongian nor a neo-Meinongian. However, I have sometimes applied certain elements of Meinongianism to the problem of fictitious objects and the theory of artifacts in general.

1. Adrian fears the devil.
2. Adrian's fear is intentionally directed toward the devil. (1; principle of intentionality)
3. The devil does not exist.
4. That which does not exist is nothing (i.e., no object).
5. Adrian fears nothing. (1, 3, 4)
6. Adrian's fear is not intentionally directed toward any object. (5)
7. Adrian's fear is not intentionally directed toward the devil. (6)

Brentano was Meinong's first and most important philosophical teacher; and Meinong was deeply impressed by Brentano's principle of intentionality. It is therefore unsurprising that Meinong strived for a solution to the puzzle of the intentional directedness toward something that does not exist. His solution was to reject assumption 4 in the above deduction. In other words, Meinong expands the notion of an object such that being an object does not entail existence. Consequently, the inference from "Adrian fears the devil" and the "The devil does not exist" to "Adrian fears nothing" is blocked, and hence the problem of intentionality is resolved.[11]

1.2.2 The Problem of Negative Singular Existence Statements

The problem of negative singular existence statements is one of the oldest puzzles in philosophy. It could be stated as follows: How can one – consistently – deny *of* something that *it* does not exist? Willard van Orman Quine calls it "Plato's beard".[12] The problem rests, among other things, on the following principle, which may be called the "composition principle": In a meaningful sentence, every (syncategorematic) component must be meaningful.[13] Taken together with a referential semantics of singular terms, this, again, leads to contradiction:

---

[11] Brentano himself, however, advocated a radically different solution: He claimed that intentionality is not a real relation, such that "S is intentionality directed toward X" does not entail that there is an object X that S is directed toward. Brentano would declare that this deduction is fallacious because the step from 1, 3, and 4 to 5 is invalid. In more recent times, a similar view can be found in Prior (1971) (chapter 8); Gorman (2006); Crane (2012 and 2013). The problem of intentionality is also discussed in Wettstein (1984); Zalta (1988); Priest (2005).

[12] Quine (1948/1953). For further discussions of the problem of negative existentials, see Lejewski (1954); Leonard (1956); Leblanc and Hailperin (1959); Zalta (1983); Perszyk (1993); Salmon (1998).

[13] In linguistics, a word is called "syncategorematic" (or "synsemantic") if it does not have a standalone denotation but contributes to the denotation of word complexes. For instance, the definite article "the" and the preposition "of" in "the Fountain of Youth" are syncategorematic expressions, while "fountain" and "youth" are so-called categorematic (or "autosemantic") expressions. The "composition principle" is related to, but not identical with, the so-called principle of compositionality, which states that the meaning of a complex expression is determined by the meanings of its constituent expressions (which would be compatible with some components having no meaning).

1. "The Fountain of Youth does not exist" is a meaningful sentence.
2. In a meaningful sentence, every (syncategorematic) component must be meaningful. (composition principle)
3. Each (syncategorematic) component of "The Fountain of Youth does not exist" is meaningful. (1, 2)
4. The meaning of a singular term, like "the Fountain of Youth", is its denotation.
5. "The Fountain of Youth does not exist" is true.
6. Thus, "the Fountain of Youth" is an empty singular term, that is, it does not have any denotation. (5)
7. "The Fountain of Youth" is not a meaningful expression. (4, 6)
8. "The Fountain of Youth does not exist" is not a meaningful sentence. (2, 7)

It can hardly be denied that there are meaningful and true negative singular existence sentences, and the composition principle seems to be highly plausible. One could try to solve the puzzle by rejecting 4 in the above deduction, that is, by denying the referential semantics of singular terms. The Meinongian solution, however, is to reject the step from 5 to 6: Meinongians deny that "The Fountain of Youth does not exist" entails that "the Fountain of Youth" is an empty singular term. In fact, according to Meinongianism, there are no empty singular terms at all (at least no empty definite descriptions). This is a consequence of CP. Thus, the problem of negative singular existentials is resolved.

1.2.3 The Problem of Fictitious Objects

The problem of intentionality and the problem of negative singular existentials are surely among the most important motives for Meinongianism. However, neo-Meinongians have applied their theories to a variety of fields, among them philosophy of time and tense, philosophy of mathematics, philosophy of science, and even philosophy of religion.[14] Moreover, Meinongianism may also be motivated by the view that sentences like "The golden mountain is golden," "The round square is a square," and "Pegasus is identical with Pegasus" are necessarily true (see Lambert, 1983: 146f.). Sometimes Meinongianism is applied to provide fresh perspectives on theories from various epochs of the history of philosophy.[15]

---

[14] For a Meinongian philosophy of religion, see Miravalle (2019). For applications to philosophy of mathematics, see Routley (1980); Jacquette (1996); Priest (2005). For philosophy of science, see Routley (1980); Jacquette (1996). For a Meinongian theory of past and future objects, see Hinchliff (1988); Salmon (1998). For an overview of various important applications, see Reicher (2022).

[15] See Castañeda (1972) on Frege and Geach; Zalta (1988) on Husserl; Parsons (1995) on the medieval discussion of sentences like "I owe you a horse"; Jacquette (1996) on Anselm's "ontological proof" for God's existence.

However, the most important field of application of Meinongianism (at least in terms of the quantity of published contributions) is the theory of fiction and fictitious objects. Characters, events, and places from fictional novels, movies, TV series, fairy tales, and myths are interpreted as Meinongian objects of one sort or another.[16]

As a first approximation, the problem of fictitious objects may be stated as follows: There seem to be true statements about fictitious objects. In particular, there are true predications about them, statements like "Pegasus is a winged horse" or "Sherlock Holmes is an extraordinarily astute detective." How can that be, given that fictitious objects do not exist (which seems to be, after all, the distinguishing mark of the fictitious)?

Fictitious objects give rise to a number of paradoxes, among them the following two.

Paradox of Fictions I:
1. Pegasus is a fictitious object.
2. Fictitious objects do not exist.
3. Pegasus does not exist. (1, 2)
4. Pegasus is a flying horse.
5. $\exists x \, (x = \text{Pegasus})$. (4, PP)

Two explanatory remarks: (1) The formula "$\exists x \, (x = a)$" is usually read as "There is something that is identical with *a*." This, in turn, is often interpreted as synonymous with "*a* exists." Given this interpretation, 5 contradicts 3. (2) The step from 4 to 5 is licensed by the following principle, which I call the *predication principle* (PP):

(PP) $Fa \rightarrow \exists x(x = a)$.[17]

PP may be read as follows: If an object *a* is F/has the property of being F, then *a* exists. The individual constant "*a*" stands for a singular term, and "F" stands for a predicate expression. Arguably, PP is intuitively very plausible (at least for most instances). Moreover, in standard predicate logic, PP is even trivially true because the right-hand term of the conditional – "$\exists x \, (x = a)$" – is a *logical truth*, and thus the conditional as a whole turns out to be true in all circumstances. That "$\exists x \, (x = a)$" is taken as logically true in standard logic is due to the fact that standard logic involves an *existence assumption with*

---

[16] See Parsons (1975 and 1980); Routley (1979 and 1980); Castañeda (1979); Fine (1982 and 1984); Zalta (1983 and 1988); Lambert (1983); Jacquette (1989 and 1996); Priest (2005 and 2011a); Berto (2008 and 2011); Sainsbury (2010): chapter 3.

[17] This is, in fact, a familiar, albeit controversial, principle. Routley calls it "the ontological assumption" (Routley (1980): chapter I, §3).

respect to singular terms. In standard logic, it is presupposed that every singular term denotes something. Nondenoting singular terms are simply not permitted.[18]

Paradox of Fictions I can be resolved in a number of ways: (1) One may reject premise 2 (i.e., deny that fictitious objects do not exist). (2) One may reject premise 4 (i.e., deny that "Pegasus is a flying horse" is true, if it is understood literally). (3) One may reject PP and thus block the step from 4 to 5. (4) One may reject the reading of "$\exists x\ (x = a)$" as "Pegasus exists."

The first solution – admitting that fictitious objects exist – is common within contemporary philosophy of fiction. The basic idea of this view is that fictitious objects are a particular kind of contingent cultural entity, *abstract artifacts*, constituents of fictional works (or stories), created by the authors of these works. This view is sometimes called *artifactualism* or *creationism*.[19] According to artifactualism, it is a mistake to treat fictitious characters as paradigm examples of nonexistent entities. Artifactualism as such does not rule out that Meinongians may assume nonexistent fictitious objects, just as they may assume nonexistent mountains, nonexistent geometrical figures, nonexistent real persons, and so on. However, Pegasus, Sherlock Holmes, and their ilk do not belong to this category.

The second solution – the denial of the literal truth of a sentence like "Pegasus is a flying horse" – comes in several varieties. Here are some of them:

(1) It is claimed that a sentence like "Pegasus is a flying horse" is an elliptical rendering of a statement which is not about Pegasus, but about something very different – for instance, a fictitious work or story, mental acts of an author or readers.[20] Of course, a statement about a fictitious work or an author's mental acts, and so on, does not entail the existence of flying horses.

(2) It is claimed that a sentence like "Pegasus is a flying horse" is an elliptical rendering of a statement that can be generated by prefixing to it a so-called

---

[18] Existence assumptions have their roots in the early history of logic and can be motivated by a general referential view of meaning, according to which nondenoting terms are not meaningful (see the previously mentioned composition principle). They have been questioned – with good reason – in so-called Free Logics (see Lambert (1983 and 1991)), but also – some decades earlier – by Polish logicians (see Lejewski (1954)). The admission of empty singular terms is also defended in Leonard (1956). More will be said about free logics in Subsections 3.4 and 5.3.

[19] To my knowledge, the first philosopher who held an artifactualist view of fictional objects was the Polish phenomenologist Roman Ingarden in his groundbreaking monograph *Das literarische Kunstwerk* (*The Literary Work of Art*, Ingarden (1931/2012)). For later developments of artifactualism, see MacDonald (1954); van Inwagen (1977); Salmon (1998); Thomasson (1999); Voltolini (2006); Abell (2020). For a criticism of artefactualism from an antirealist point of view, see Yagisawa (2001); Sainsbury (2010): chapter 5; Kroon (2011).

[20] See Braithwaite (1933); Ryle (1933); Bach (1985–1986); Kapitan (1990).

story operator, that is, a locution like "according to a story" or "according to Greek mythology", and so on.[21] Since the story operator is interpreted as a *sentence* operator (structurally similar to "it is possible that", "it has been the case that", "it is desirable that"), one cannot deduce that there are flying horses from "According to a story: Pegasus is a flying horse," but (at best): "According to a story: There are flying horses."

(3) It is claimed that a statement like "Pegasus is a flying horse" is usually uttered in a particular mode of discourse, in which it is understood among the participants that the statement is not to be taken seriously.[22] This is sometimes called the *theory of pretense*. The idea is that participants in fictional discourse – and also in discourse about fiction – behave like actors on a stage. Just as actors in a play do not really love, fight, murder, and so on, but only *pretend* to do so, the participants in fictional discourse and discourse about fiction pretend to talk about winged horses, and so on. They engage, as it were, in a particular "game of make-believe". For instance, within the make-believe game of Greek mythology, Pegasus is a flying horse. Accordingly, within this game, there are flying horses. However, since the make-believe facts of the Greek mythology game do not spill over to reality, there is no contradiction to the "serious" statement that there are no flying horses.

The third solution to Paradox of Fictions I – rejecting PP – also has prominent proponents.[23] Meinongians, however, usually choose the fourth option, that is, rejecting the "existential" reading of "$\exists x\,(x = a)$". As already mentioned, one of the basic tenets of Meinongianism is that there is a difference between "there is" and "exists", and that the former does not entail the latter. Most Meinongians use the quantifier "$\exists x$" to express "there is" – instead of "exists". Consequently, "$\exists x\,(x = \text{Pegasus})$" is not interpreted as "Pegasus exists," but as "There is something that is (identical with) Pegasus," where the latter does not imply the former. Therefore, the bottom line of the above deduction – "$\exists x\,(x = \text{Pegasus})$" – is not in conflict with 3 ("Pegasus does not exist"). Thus, the paradox is resolved – or rather, it is shown that there is no paradox in the first place. It just turns out that there are objects that do not exist (which is, after all, what Meinongians are eager to show), and that Pegasus belongs to this category.

---

[21] See Bertolet (1984); Künne (1990). A structurally similar solution has been proposed in Brock (2002). However, Brock's sentence operator is not "According to a story . . . " but "According to the realist hypothesis . . . ". Brock calls this position "fictionalism about fictional characters".

[22] See Currie (1990); Walton (1990); Everett (2005 and 2013).

[23] See Leblanc and Hailperin (1959); Barnes (1972: chapter 3); Crittenden (1973); Lambert (1983); Azzouni (2013).

Paradox of Fictions II:

1. $\neg\exists x$ (x is a flying horse). (Read: There are no flying horses, or: Flying horses do not exist.)
2. Pegasus is a flying horse.
3. $\exists x$ (x is a flying horse). (2, EG) (Read: There are flying horses; or: There is at least one flying horse; or: Flying horses exist.)

3 obviously contradicts 1. The step from 2 to 3 is licensed by the so-called principle of existential generalization (EG):

(EG) $Fa \rightarrow \exists x Fx$.
(Read: If a is F, then there is/exists something that is F.)

Existential generalization is, again, intuitively very plausible (at least in most contexts), and it is one of the basic principles of standard logic.[24]

Various proposals were made to resolve paradoxes of this sort. Again, a natural move is to deny the – literal – truth of "Pegasus is a flying horse." An alternative is to reject EG, that is, to claim that "a is F" does not imply "There is something that is F."[25] However, Meinongians do not need to give up EG. They can simply point out – as with the first paradox of fiction – that the quantifier does not express existence but rather the weaker "there is", and that, therefore, "There are flying horses" does not contradict "Flying horses do not exist." Meinongians share with the rest of us the belief that flying horses do not exist, but they hold that there are flying horses (with Pegasus being one of them). Thus, Meinongians can accept the conclusion of the above deduction as true. In this case, they have to reject its negation, 1: $\neg\exists x$ (x is a flying horse). Meinongians can do so consistently by pointing out that this string of symbols is not a correct rendering of the natural language sentence "Flying horses do not exist."

1.3 A Very Brief History

Meinong's theory of objects has had a chequered history. In Germanophone philosophy, it basically disappeared after Meinong's death. This was partly due to the fervent opposition of the Brentano school, but also to the fact that Meinong's disciple and follower Ernst Mally turned his back on object theory in his later years (although he had made very important contributions to its development).

---

[24] However, EG has been rejected not only by avowed Meinongians, but also by a number of logicians in the 1950s without explicit reference to Meinong. See Leonard (1956); Leblanc and Hailperin (1959); Rescher (1959).

[25] For this move, see Leonard (1956); Leblanc and Hailperin (1959).

In Anglophone philosophy, at the beginning of the twentieth century, Meinong's object theory was received almost exclusively through Bertrand Russell's comments.[26] Russell, though originally sympathetic to Meinong's theory, put forward two (seemingly devastating) objections against it in his seminal paper "On Denoting" (1905). For decades, Russell's criticism determined the assessment of object theory in analytic philosophy. A pointed formulation of the mainstream view up to the 1970s is the following infamous judgment of Gilbert Ryle: "Let us frankly concede from the start that *Gegenstandstheorie* itself is dead, buried and not going to be resurrected" (Ryle, 1973: 255).

In 1933, the South African philosopher John N. Findlay submitted a dissertation at the University of Graz (supervised by Ernst Mally), originally published as *Meinong's Theory of Objects* and, in the second edition, as *Meinong's Theory of Objects and Values* (Findlay, 1963). For a long time, this book was the main source on Meinong's theory for Anglophone philosophers.

The first sympathetic treatment of object theory after Findlay's dissertation was Roderick M. Chisholm's paper "Beyond Being and Nonbeing" (1972). In the following decades, Meinong's object theory was revived by a number of philosophers and logicians who worked on its consistent logical reconstruction and tried to show that it is a viable option, with a number of fruitful and important applications (see Section 5). Today, Meinongianism is perhaps livelier than ever, defended in a variety of versions and taken seriously by its opponents.

2 Logical Issues Raised by Basic Meinongian Principles

The basic principles of Meinongianism, in particular M and CP, raise a number of logical issues. To begin with, how should one represent its main thesis,

(M) There are objects that do not exist,

in logical notation? If, as Quine has it, "[e]xistence is what the existential quantifier expresses" (Quine, 1969: 97), M turns out to be nonsensical and not expressible in a well-formed logical formula. In M, "exist" is used as a predicate expression, but in Quinean logic it must not be treated as a predicate. It is expressed exclusively by means of the existential quantifier. Thus, in the formal language of Quinean logic, M cannot be expressed. This issue will be dealt with in Subsection 2.1.

Further logical concerns arise from the characterization principle (CP), according to which, for every set of properties, there is a corresponding object, either an existent or a nonexistent one, which has all and only the properties in the set (see Subsection 1.1). This seems to entail an infringement of the

---

[26] But see also Hicks (1922). (My attention was drawn to this reference by Johann Marek.)

principle of excluded middle (Subsection 2.2) and the principle of noncontradiction (Subsection 2.3). Moreover, CP raises a problem that may be called "the paradox of simplicity" (Subsection 2.4).

2.1 The Distinction between "There Is" ("∃x") and "Exists" ("E!")

To make sense of M ("There are objects that do not exist"), one needs to distinguish between "*There are* objects that are such-and-such" and "Objects that are such-and-such *exist*." However, standard logical notation (with the quantifier "∃x" as the sole symbol for expressing "there is" as well as "exist") does not provide the means for such a distinction.

There are two possible reactions to this. The Quinean reaction is to declare M – even in its natural language formulation – to be nonsensical. For a Quinean, the formal language of standard logic (which allows us to express existence solely by means of the quantifier) is perfectly adequate. The impossibility of expressing M in this formal language is just a symptom of M's being nonsensical in the first place. For a Quinean, the distinction between "there are Fs" and "Fs exist" simply does not make sense.

For a Meinongian, however, it is the other way around: A Meinongian considers the distinction between "there is" and "exists" as a basic metaphysical distinction. If this distinction cannot be expressed in a given formal language, this is considered to be a shortfall of the formal language.

Meinongians and Quineans agree, in principle, that a formal language should be as clear and simple as possible. They also agree that a formal language should have maximum expressive power, that is, it should – ideally – allow for the symbolic representation of any meaningful natural language expression. This should be possible in a way that does justice to important distinctions that can be expressed in natural languages. In the case of M, the disagreement concerns the question of whether M is a meaningful sentence in the first place.

Since Meinongians answer this question affirmatively, they consider it a shortfall of standard logical notation that it does not allow for a formal rendering of M. The usual remedy for this shortfall is the addition of an existence predicate to the vocabulary of the symbolic language. Most neo-Meinongian logicians make use of an existence predicate (mostly represented as "E!" or simply "E") in their formal language.[27] This is a natural consequence

---

[27] See Rescher (1959); Cocchiarella (1969): §3; Rapaport (1978): section 6; Parsons (1980); Routley (1980); Zalta (1983 and 1988); Lambert (1991); Jacquette (1996); Paśniczek (1998): section 3.3; Priest (2005); Berto (2013): section 7.6. An exception is Hector-Neri Castañeda: He defines singular existence statements ("*x* exists") by using the concept of self-identity (Castañeda (1972): section 5). "E!" is also used in Leonard (1956).

of the doctrine that there are objects that do not exist. At the same time, it is a serious deviation from standard logics. The use of "E!" allows for representing M in logical notation as follows:

(M') $\exists x(\neg E!x)$.

Ever since Kant's famous critique of Anselm's so-called ontological proof of God's existence,[28] however, philosophical mainstream has it that existence is *not* a logical predicate. The most perspicuous rendering of this view is to be found in Gottlob Frege (1891, 1892a, 2021a, and 2021b), which is the source of the previously mentioned Quinean postulate that existence is what the quantifier expresses. According to the Kant–Frege doctrine of existence, the introduction of an existence predicate in a formal language is a gross mistake, since it is in deep conflict with the very nature of existence.

In defense of the Meinongian view, one could argue that standard, Quinean logical notation does not only lack the power to express the controversial metaphysical principle M. Perhaps the much more serious failure is that standard logical notation does not allow for a symbolic rendering of singular existence statements – at least not in a straightforward manner.

The problem concerns positive and negative singular existence statements (see Subsection 1.2.2) alike. Consider, for instance, the following exchange: "God exists." – "No, God does not exist."[29] Although it may be difficult to assign a truth value to either statement, both of them seem to be perfectly meaningful – as theists, atheists, and agnostics agree. But rendering them in standard logical notation proves difficult. Given that existence is expressed by the existential quantifier, a beginner in symbolic logic might expect that "God exists" could be rendered as follows: (G*) $\exists x (g)$, where "*g*" is an individual constant that stands for the (alleged) proper name "God". However, G* is not a well-formed formula because the quantifier "$\exists x$" must be followed by a predicate expression ("F*x*", "G*x*" etc.) in order to yield a complete and well-formed existential quantification. It is not permitted to put an individual constant at the place of the predicate – as in G*.

---

[28] The famous passage in Kant's *Critique of Pure Reason* (1787/1929, B 627) goes as follows: "'Being' is obviously not a real predicate; that is, it is not a concept of something which could be added to the concept of a thing." However, Kant develops his view on existence much more perspicuously in his "Der einzig mögliche Beweisgrund zu einer Demonstration des Daseyns Gottes" ("The sole possible argument for a demonstration of God's existence," 1763/2011). In this essay, it becomes clear that Kant's view is astonishingly close to Frege's.

[29] I take it for granted, in the context of this example, that "God" is a singular term. Sometimes this is called into question. I will not enter this debate here. Readers who are worried about this particular example may replace "God" with "Zeus" or "Pegasus" or "Atlantis" or whatever they like.

Quineans do not deny that there are meaningful singular existence statements in natural languages. Thus, on pain of having to admit that their formal language has inadequately poor expressive power, they are pressed to find a way of somehow expressing such statements in their logical notation. A simple solution would be to make use of complex predicates of the form "= a" (read: "is identical with a"), where "a" is a singular term.[30] Accordingly, "God exists" could be rendered as $(G^1) \exists x \, (x = g)$. (Read: There is an x, such that x is identical with God.) However, as pointed out above, the negation of "$\exists x \, (x = g)$" is logically false in classical logic because standard logic involves an existence assumption with respect to singular terms. Therefore, this option is not available to Quineans who want to allow for the possibility that "$\exists x \, (x = g)$" is false. Alternatively, one might do without the identity sign and simply take an arbitrary predicate constant (say, "G"), which could be taken to stand for the complex natural language predicate "is identical with God". If one chooses this option, "God exists" can be rendered as $(G^2) \, \exists x \, (Gx)$.[31] Either way, the (grammatical) singular existence statement "God exists" has been transformed into a general existence statement "There is an x, such that $x \ldots$."

There is still another option, which makes use of Bertrand Russell's theory of definite descriptions, combined with a descriptive theory of proper names.[32] Consider (to use Russell's original example): (K) "The present king of France is bald." Since there is no present king of France, the definite description "the present king of France" is an empty singular term. If (as the reference theory has it) the meaning of a term is its denotation, and if (as the composition principle states) in a meaningful sentence, every component must be meaningful, K turns out to be meaningless (see Subsection 1.2.2) – which may seem counterintuitive.

Russell's problem was related to this, but not exactly the same: He was worried about a looming "truth value gap". If there is no present king of France, it seems that one can neither affirm nor deny that he is bald. Hence it seems that K is neither true nor false, which struck Russell as hard to swallow. His solution was to interpret K in the following way: (K^R) There is exactly one

---

[30] The vocabulary of standard logical notation does not contain an identity sign, but it is simple and unproblematic to add "=" to it. Logic with identity is called an *extension* of standard logic. The extension with identity is quite uncontroversial – in contrast to extensions with the existence predicate "E!".

[31] Cf. Quine's artificial predicate "pegasizes", which is equivalent with "is identical with Pegasus" (Quine (1948/1953)).

[32] Russell develops his theory of definite descriptions in "On Denoting" (1905a). The theory of definite descriptions was extremely influential, but it did not go uncontested. For a prominent criticism, see Strawson (1950). Russell also holds a descriptive theory of proper names (see Russell (1910–1911): 114–116; Russell (1918–1919): Lecture VI), along with Gottlob Frege (1892b/2021). The descriptive theory of proper names is sometimes called the Frege–Russell theory of proper names.

x, such that *x* is a king of France, and *x* is bald. Thus, Russell analyzed sentence K, which has the grammatical structure of a predication, as a complex existence quantification. Since it is false that there is exactly one *x*, such that *x* is a king of France (because there is no king of France), the whole complex is false. The truth value gap is avoided.

Russell's theory of definite descriptions can also be used to resolve the problem of singular existence statements. Consider: "The present king of France does not exist." A Russellian analysis of this looks as follows: "It is not the case that there is exactly one present king of France."[33] According to this analysis, the seeming singular existence statement turns out to be a general existence statement, that is, an existential quantification.

Russell's theory of definite descriptions may work well for definite descriptions, but what about proper names such as "Pegasus", "Atlantis", and so on? If a singular existence statement contains a proper name in its subject position (as in "Atlantis does not exist"), Russell's analysis cannot be applied, at least not directly. In order to make the theory of definite descriptions applicable to such cases, one has to substitute a definite description for the proper name, for example, "the winged horse from Greek mythology" for "Pegasus". Russell indeed thought that proper names are "truncated descriptions" (Russell, 1918–1919: 208) or "abbreviations for descriptions" (Russell, 1918–1919: 524), such that a substitution of a definite description for a proper name is always possible and unproblematic. However, this so-called descriptive theory of proper names is controversial – and with good reason.[34] To mention just one of its well-known problems, consider the sentence: "Pegasus is the winged horse from Greek mythology." Given that "Pegasus" is short for the definite description "the winged horse from Greek mythology", this would turn out as the tautological truth "The winged horse from Greek mythology is the winged horse from Greek mythology." However, the original sentence does not seem to be trivially true.

To sum up: Quineans *do* have resources to account for the truth of singular existence statements, but one may feel that their proposals are somewhat awkward. Either they have to work with artificial predicate expressions (like "is identical with Pegasus" or "pegasizes"), or they have to rely on a controversial theory of proper names.

Meinongians, on the other hand, have no problem with singular existence statements in the first place. Their symbolic rendering of "God does not exist," for example, is simply and straightforwardly "¬E!*g*" (where "*g*" stands for the singular term "God"). Meinongians do not have to paraphrase grammatical

---

[33] In a half-formal rendering: ¬(∃*x* (*x* is a king of France) ∧ ∀*y* (*y* is a king of France → *y* = *x*)).

[34] The most prominent attack on the descriptive theory of proper names is Kripke (1980). For an overview of the debate and numerous other sources, see Cumming (2019).

singular existence statements into general existence statements, they do not have to introduce artificial predicate expressions, and they can do justice to the distinction between definite descriptions and proper names. This seems to be a point in favor of Meinongianism, or, more exactly: a point in favor of the distinction between "there is" (the quantifier, "$\exists x$") and "exists" (the predicate, "E!").

2.2 Meinongianism and the Principle of Excluded Middle

Consider, for instance, the object The Blue, that is, the object that has the property of being blue as its sole determination (i.e., the object that corresponds to the set that has the property of being blue as its sole element). According to CP, this object does not have any shape, any size, does not consist of any particular material, is not located anywhere in space, and so on. According to CP, it holds, among other things, that neither "The Blue is round" nor "The Blue is not round" is true. This seems to contradict the principle of excluded middle (PEM), which states that, for every proposition p, either p or non-p is true.

This can be generalized in the following way: It is a consequence of CP that most nonexistent objects are, as Meinong pointedly puts it, "incompletely determined" or, in short: "incomplete" objects. This means (in most cases) that, if x is a nonexistent object, then, for some general term φ, neither "x is φ" is true nor "x is not φ" is true (Meinong, 1915/1972: §25).[35] Thus, (most) nonexistent objects seem to violate PEM.

Meinong observes that incomplete determination (in short, incompleteness) is indeed a peculiarity of nonexistent objects: Existent objects (both real and ideal ones) are always completely determined.[36] That is, for any existent object x (be it real or ideal) and any φ, it holds, without restriction: Either x is φ or x is not φ (Meinong, 1915/1972: §25).

Meinong notes that incomplete objects seem to violate PEM – and he readily accepts this violation. He states that PEM is valid only under the presupposition of complete determination. Incomplete objects simply fall outside its scope (Meinong, 1915/1972: §25).

---

[35] I use "φ" as a *variable for general terms*, i.e., for expressions that form, together with the copula "is", a complete predicate (i.e., expressions like "blue", "round", "a mountain", etc.). General-term variables must be clearly distinguished from the individual variables x, y, z etc. In contrast to individual variables, general-term variables must not be replaced by names (not even by names for general terms!) but rather by general terms. General-term variables are one of several kinds of *nonnominal* variables, i.e., variables that do not stand in for *nomina*. For the use of nonnominal variables, see Prior (1971). In standard (Quinean) logic, only individual variables occur. The use of variables of other kinds is not permitted. This restriction is closely related to the Quinean doctrine that the quantifier "$\exists x$" expresses existence, since, if "$\exists x$" expresses existence, the use of other than individual variables would yield nonsense.

[36] For Meinong's distinction between real and ideal objects, see Subsection 1.1.

However, as closer inspection shows, there is no need to restrict the validity of PEM to complete objects only. One may argue that incomplete objects do not violate PEM, if the principle is properly conceived. This claim is based on a distinction between two kinds of negation, namely external and internal negation. External negation is *sentence (proposition) negation*. This is how negation, in standard logics, is usually conceived: The negator has a complete assertive statement ("F*a*", in the simplest case) within its scope. Internal negation, by contrast, is *predicate negation*: The internal negator has only the predicate term within its scope. In the example at the beginning of this subsection, the distinction between internal and external negation is the distinction between "It is not the case that the Blue is round" and "The Blue is non-round." The former expresses (in terms of property exemplification) that The Blue does not exemplify the property of being round. The latter expresses that The Blue does exemplify *the negative property* of being non-round.[37]

In logical notation, predicate negation can be distinguished from sentence negation either by using distinct symbols for each or by using the same symbol in a distinct grammatical structure. One might use "¬" for sentence negation and "~" for predication negation – or the other way around. For instance, "It is not the case that The Blue is round, and it is not the case that The Blue is non-round" can be represented in the following way: $\neg(Rb) \wedge \neg(\sim Rb)$. Alternatively, one might render this as follows: $\sim(bR) \wedge \sim(b\sim R)$ (see Routley, 1980: 89). Often, negative predicates are symbolized as $\overline{F}, \overline{G}, \overline{H} \ldots$, in contrast to F, G, H ... Accordingly, the previously mentioned sentence would be represented as: $\neg Rb \wedge \neg \overline{R}b$. It does not matter which of these alternatives is chosen (and which symbols are used). It is important, however, to note that neo-Meinongians like Routley and Jacquette adhere to the following principles:

$\neg\forall x(\overline{F}x \leftrightarrow \neg Fx)$.

(Read: It is not the case that, for all x: x is non-F if, and only if, it is not the case that x is F. For instance, it is not the case that The Triangle has the property of being red. But from this, we cannot deduce that The Triangle has the negative property of being non-red.)

$\neg\forall x(\overline{F}x \vee Fx)$.

(For instance, The Triangle neither has the property of being right-angled nor the property of being non-right-angled.)

$\exists x(Fx \wedge \overline{F}x)$.

(For instance, The Round Square has the property of being round as well as the property of being non-round.)

---

[37] Interestingly, Meinong is well aware of the distinction between internal and external negation, and he even explicitly notes that PEM is unrestrictedly valid if one conceives of it in the sense of external (or, as he calls it, "extended") negation. (Meinong (1915/1972): §25) But he obviously interprets the negation in PEM as internal, and thus he cannot take this way out.

As long as we are only concerned with existent objects, the distinction between internal and external negation may easily escape our attention. This is because, for existent objects, it is hardly relevant. Take an arbitrary material object, say, my desk: Since it is not the case that my desk is round, it is also the case that my desk is non-round. Analogous considerations seem to hold for any existent object and any predicate. However, as soon as we take nonexistent objects into account, the distinction becomes immensely relevant. Consider again The Blue: While The Blue is indeed neither round nor non-round, it is nevertheless true that it is not the case that The Blue is round. Moreover, it is not the case that The Blue is non-round.

As it is usually conceived, PEM involves *external* negation. That is, it says that, for all x, and all φ: Either x is φ, or it is not the case that x is φ. As can be seen from the reasoning in the previous paragraph, The Blue does not violate this principle. For it holds indeed, for all φ, that either The Blue is φ, or it is not the case that the Blue is φ. If we insert the predicate expression "blue" for "φ" in "The Blue is φ," we get a true sentence, since it is the case that The Blue is blue. With all other possible insertions ("round", "rectangular", "wooden", "iron" ...), we get a false sentence, since The Blue is neither round nor rectangular, neither wooden nor iron, and so on. Analogous reasoning holds for every incompletely determined object x: For any φ, if being φ belongs to the determinations of x, it is the case that x is φ, and if being φ does not belong to the determinations of x, it is not the case that x is φ. So far, incomplete objects behave exactly like complete ones. The difference comes to the fore as soon as we consider internal negation: While, for complete objects, usually "It is not the case that x is φ" implies "It is the case that x is non-φ," this implication does not hold for incomplete objects.

Now it is clear that Meinongianism need not be in conflict with PEM. If PEM is understood as the principle that, for every p, either p or the external negation of p must be true, no conflict arises. "The Blue is not round" can be read either externally or internally, that is, as "It is not the case that The Blue is round" or as "The Blue is non-round." The former (the external negation) is true, while the latter (the internal negation) is false. It is true that The Blue is neither round nor non-round; but this is compatible with PEM. PEM only requires that either The Blue is round, or it is not the case that The Blue is round. Since it is indeed not the case that The Blue is round, PEM applies to The Blue without restriction.

2.3 Meinongianism and the Principle of Noncontradiction

Consider, for instance, the object The Round Square. As Russell famously noted, objects of this kind seem to contradict the principle of noncontradiction

(PNC). For, according to CP, The Round Square is both round and a square; and, under the plausible assumption that being a square entails being non-round, both "The Round Square is round" and "The Round Square is non-round" are true – which is ruled out by PNC. (Russell, 1905a and 1905b) Of course, by Russell's lights, this would be reason enough to reject Meinongianism.

Meinong was unimpressed by this objection: He replied that PNC was designed for the domain of existent and possible objects only, and that it is therefore not surprising that it does not hold for impossible objects as well (Meinong, 1907/1973: §3).

But was Meinong perhaps too quick to admit the violation of PNC in his reply to Russell? There is an alternative rejoinder that, again, relies on the distinction between internal and external negation: Clearly, PNC is to be understood in an external manner. It says that for any proposition p, it cannot be the case that both "p" and "$\neg p$" are true. From this, it follows that there is no x such that both "x is round" and "It is not the case that x is round" are true. However, The Round Square does not violate PNC, thus understood. For the statement "The Round Square is round" is true, and its external negation – "It is not the case that The Round Square is round" – is false. In the same vein, the statement "The Round Square is non-round" is true and its external negation is false. "The Round Square is not round" is ambiguous between "The Round Square is non-round" (predicate negation) and "It is not the case that the Round Square is round" (sentence negation). "The Round Square is non-round" does not imply "It is not the case that the Round Square is round." The impression that The Round Square violates PNC can arise only if one ignores the distinction between the external negation "It is not the case that The Round Square is round" and the internal negation "The Round Square is non-round."[38]

However, Russell has a second objection up his sleeve: According to CP, there is not only The Round Square but also The Existent Round Square; and, again according to CP, just as The Round Square is round and a square, The Existent Round Square is not only round and a square, but it also exists (Russell, 1905a and 1905b). This is, of course, a problem for Meinong, because he is not prepared to accept that something that is both round and a square exists.

Meinong himself considers this the more serious challenge for object theory. He observes that this objection does not only apply to impossible objects, like The Round Square, but also to possible ones, like The Golden Mountain. For,

---

[38] This Meinongian rejoinder is proposed in Griffin (1985–1986). However, Griffin points out that Russell's objection can be sharpened such that this way out is no longer possible. For it seems that, according to CP, there is not only an object that is both round and non-round, but also an object that is both round and such that it is not the case that it is round (Ibid.: 392–394).

according to CP, there is not only The Golden Mountain but also The Existent Golden Mountain, and The Existent Golden Mountain is not just golden and a mountain but also existent (Meinong, 1907/1973: §3). However, according to Meinong's theory of objects, The Existent Golden Mountain no more exists than does The Golden Mountain. Thus, even if one puts aside impossible objects, object theory seems to be inconsistent.

Meinong counters this objection by claiming that there is a semantic difference between "The Existent Golden Mountain *exists*" and "The Existent Golden Mountain *is existent*" and that, while the latter is true, the former is false (Meinong, 1907: §3). Russell dismisses this rejoinder as incomprehensible (Russell, 1907). This was the end of the debate between Russell and Meinong.

It was not, however, the end of the debate between Meinongians and Anti-Meinongians. As we shall see in Section 4, Meinong's distinction between being existent and existing is not the desperate ad hoc maneuver that it may seem to be at first glance. Moreover, neo-Meinongians have developed a variety of strategies to resolve the paradox of The Existent Golden Mountain (see Subsection 5.4).

2.4 Remaining Problems

Even if one accepts the Meinongian solutions outlined in the previous subsections, a number of problems remain. There is still the problem of The Existent Golden Mountain, for which it has yet to be shown that Meinong's distinction between existing and being existent can provide a viable solution.

Furthermore, there is *the paradox of simplicity*: According to CP, it is true of the object The Blue that it has being blue as its sole property. However, this seems to entail that The Blue has in fact (at least) *two* properties, namely being blue and having exactly one property, which seems to contradict the postulate that it has being blue as its sole property.[39]

Moreover, the Meinongian interpretation of existence as a predicate is highly controversial, and it is still unclear what the quantifier "$\exists x$" is supposed to express if it does not express existence. This question will be discussed in the next section.

The problem of The Existent Golden Mountain will be taken up again in Section 4, where a refinement and extension of Meinongianism will be presented, and it will be shown that it has the resources to solve this problem. It will also be shown that the same extension provides a solution to the paradox of simplicity.

---

[39] Meinong himself raises this problem, albeit with a slightly different example (Meinong (1915/1972): §25, 175f.).

3 Interpretations of the Quantifier "∃x"

3.1 Modes of Being versus Ontological Neutrality

As noted in Section 1, one of the basic tenets of Meinongianism is a distinction between "there is" and "exists". The relationship between "there is" and "exists" is as follows: If entities that are F (in short, Fs) exist, then there are Fs. However, the reverse does not hold: From "There are Fs" one may not infer "Fs exist." For instance, from "Black swans exist" one may infer "There are black swans." However, from "There are black swans" one may not infer "Black swans exist."[40] In principle, analogous reasoning holds for singular existence sentences, although in this context, the use of "there is" is uncommon and sounds odd.[41] However, regardless of the linguistic oddity, from "(A particular thing) *a* exists," one may infer "There is *a*." But from "There is *a*," one may not infer "*a* exists." For instance, from "God exists" one may infer "There is God." But from "There is God," one may not infer "God exists."

As noted in Section 2, in Meinongian logics, "there is" is usually expressed by means of the quantifier "∃x", while "exists" is represented as a predicate letter (commonly "E" or "E!") in symbolic notation.[42] Accordingly, "Fs exist" (e.g., "Black swans exist") can be rendered in logical notation as "$\exists x (Fx \wedge E!x)$". This implies, trivially, "$\exists xFx$" (e.g., "There are black swans"). However, "$\exists xFx$" does not imply "$\exists x (Fx \wedge E!x)$". "*a* exists" (e.g., "Pegasus exists") is rendered as "E!*a*". "There is *a*" (e.g., "There is Pegasus") may be symbolized as "$\exists x (x = a)$"; and "E!*a*" implies "$\exists x (x = a)$", but "$\exists x (x = a)$" does not imply "E!*a*".

The logical relationship between "∃x" and "E!" is quite clear. However, the distinction between "∃x" and "E!" raises further questions, notably the following: If the quantifier "∃x" does not express existence, what else does it express? What is expressed by "Black swans exist" that is not expressed by "There are black swans"? Is there really a semantic difference between "There is something that is identical with Pegasus" and "Pegasus exists"? If so, what exactly does it consist in?

Before considering various answers to these questions, it should be noted that the interpretation of "∃x" is discussed not only within Meinongianism or

---

[40] However, as an anonymous reviewer pointed out to me, a Meinongian has to admit that the entailment relation between "exist" and "there is" does not hold unrestrictedly. In particular, it does not hold for "comparative quantification", as, e.g., in: "There exist more tigers than lions" and "There are more tigers than lions" because, for a Meinongian, there must be indefinitely many tigers as well as indefinitely many lions – even if the number of existent tigers is bigger than the number of existent lions.

[41] However, different natural languages behave differently in this regard. The literal German translation of "There is God" would be "Es gibt Gott," which is grammatically sound.

[42] However, some neo-Meinongians use "∃x" to express existence and introduce a second quantifier to express the ontologically neutral "there is" (see note 55).

Meinongian logics. Rather, it is a fundamental problem of the philosophy of logic in general. However, it becomes particularly pertinent for those logics that have an existence predicate "E!" in addition to the quantifier "∃x" in their vocabulary.

There are, in principle, two possible explanations for the alleged difference between "∃x" and "E!". I call them *the modes of being view* and *the ontological neutrality view*, respectively. According to the modes of being view, there are various modes of being, with existence being just one of them. In light of this view, one may assume that nonexistent objects have a different kind of being, distinct from existence, but nevertheless a kind of being. Thus conceived, "being" is a generic concept. Furthermore, one may assume that the quantifier "∃x" just expresses this generic concept of being. Accordingly, "∃xFx" expresses that at least one F has some kind of being or other (perhaps existence, but not necessarily so); "∃x (x=a)" expresses that the particular entity *a* has some kind of being (either existence or something else).

Consequently, according to the modes of being view, the use of the quantifier "∃x" is – to use a familiar phrase – "ontologically committing" (or "ontologically loaded", as it is sometimes called). That is to say, whenever a person S claims truth for an existential quantification (say, something of the form "∃xFx"), S implicitly assumes entities of a certain sort in her ontological framework (S is ontologically committed to Fs). For instance, assume that S subscribes to the statement "There is a prime number bigger than 100," and S is apt to render this by means of the quantifier "∃x" in symbolic notation as follows: "∃x (x is a number, and x is prime, and x is bigger than 100)." Obviously, this implies "∃x (x is a number)." According to the modes of being view, S is ontologically committed to numbers. In other words, by accepting "∃x (x is a number)" as true, S implicitly admits numbers in her ontological framework. Thus, S cannot claim, on pain of inconsistency, that there is a prime number bigger than 100 and, in the same breath, deny that there are numbers, that is, deny that numbers have being of some sort (say, because numbers are abstract objects and S believes that there are only concrete objects).

Suppose S is a mathematician and a philosopher. As a mathematician, S believes that there are prime numbers bigger than 100. As a philosopher, however, S is a materialist, and she sees no way to interpret numbers as material entities. Therefore, as a philosopher, S denies that there are numbers. Thus, according to the modes of being view, a materialist philosopher-mathematician easily gets into a conflict between her philosophical views and her mathematical knowledge.

Conflicts of this sort are not only threatening to mathematicians. Linguists, literary theorists, even physicists, may easily run into similar predicaments. Just as mathematicians are likely to accept as true existential quantifications over numbers, literary theorists are likely to accept existential quantifications over fictitious characters. However, a philosophically educated literary theorist should be aware of the various paradoxes of fiction (see Section 1) and thus may come to the view that fictitious objects do not have any kind of being whatsoever. Similarly, physicists are likely to accept as true existential quantifications over "theoretical entities" such as the ideal gas. However, from a philosophical point of view, those physicists may tend to deny that entities of this sort have being. According to the modes of being view of quantification, all of these cases involve inconsistency.

By contrast, according to the ontological neutrality view, the quantifier "∃x" does not express any kind of being whatsoever. Accordingly, the acceptance of an existential quantification is not ontologically committing in any sense. In other words, the quantifier "∃x" is not ontologically loaded in any way. A mathematician-philosopher may well believe that there is a prime number bigger than 100 – in the sense of "∃x (x is a number, and x is prime, and x is bigger than 100)" – and at the same time deny that numbers have some kind of being, without being entangled in any inconsistency. Similarly, a literary theorist may claim that there are fictitious characters that are such-and-such and in the same breath reject any ontological commitment to fictitious entities. The same applies to the physicist and the ideal gas, and so forth.

Often advocates of the ontological neutrality view of the quantifier hold (implicitly or explicitly) that there is an ambiguity in the natural language expression "there is": In one sense, "there is" is the natural language equivalent to the quantifier, and in that sense, "there is" is ontological neutral (i.e., non-committing, not ontologically loaded). In another sense, "there is" may well be used to express an ontological commitment. In that sense, it is not ontologically neutral but ontologically loaded. If used in the latter sense, it must not be represented by means of the quantifier "∃x" in symbolic notation.

The claim that the English "there is" (and the corresponding expression in other natural languages) is ambiguous in this way suggests itself because it seems obvious – even to defenders of the neutrality view of the quantifier – that natural language speakers sometimes *want* to talk in an ontological committing way. Apparently, at least sometimes, they use "there is" (or its cognates in other natural languages) for this task.[43] This is clearly the case in certain philosophical contexts: When, for instance, Platonists claim that *there are* universals and nominalists deny this, "there are" is obviously meant in an ontologically committing way – for this is just what the whole debate is about. Platonists

---

[43] For an excellent discussion of ontologically committing "there is" sentences, see Peters (2008): section 6.3.

want to commit themselves to the assumption that universals belong to the realm of being, while nominalists reject this commitment. The same holds for the debates between moral realists and antirealists, psychophysical dualists and materialists, and so forth.

But ontologically committing talk occurs not only within philosophy, but in all kinds of scientific and everyday contexts. If entomologists and epidemiologists state that, recently, tiger mosquitos have been found in Western Europe, one can hardly doubt that they, in this context, understand "there are" in a robust ontological sense. (Otherwise, it would not make sense to recommend measures against the spread of tiger mosquitos in order to avoid infections with the dengue fever.) Similarly, if one states that there is apple juice in the fridge, and so forth. However, according to ontological neutralism, this kind of (ontologically committing) talk cannot be expressed by means of "$\exists x$", at least not by means of "$\exists x$" alone.

Advocates of ontological neutralism shy away from using the term "existence quantifier" or "existential quantifier" for "$\exists x$", because it would suggest an "existential" (i.e., ontological) reading. Therefore, some prefer to call it "e-quantifier". Others use the term "particularizer". The latter is meant to suggest that "$\exists x$" should be read as "For some x, ... " or "For at least one x, ... " instead of "There is an x ...." Hence, "$\exists x Fx$" is not supposed to be read as "There are Fs" or "There is something that is F," but rather as "Some x is F" or "At least one x is F."

It is important to understand that the distinction between the modes of being view and the ontological neutrality view is not a matter of logical syntax or of logical inference rules, but a matter of the *philosophical interpretation* of the logical constant "$\exists x$". Modes of being theorists and ontological neutrality theorists may use the same logical vocabulary, the same logical syntax, and the same inference rules. From the point of view of pure symbolic logic, it doesn't matter whether "$\exists x$" is read as "There is ... ", or even "There exist ... ", or rather as "Some x ... ". It is solely from a philosophical (more exactly: ontological) point of view that this issue becomes relevant. It concerns the relation between natural language expressions and logical symbols, as well as the relation between language in general and systems of beliefs/theories and reality.

3.2 Varieties of the Ontological Neutrality View

In the preceding subsection, it was pointed out that the quantifier may be interpreted as existentially loaded (ontologically committing) or as ontologically neutral, that is, noncommitting. The question of how the quantifier is to be interpreted is particularly salient for Meinongians, since they (typically) use an existence predicate in addition to the quantifier. This raises the question of whether the quantifier is supposed to express another kind of being besides existence (in which case it would be ontologically committing) or no being at all (in which case it would be ontologically neutral). In order to better understand what is at stake here, it is helpful to consider some of the most influential varieties of the ontological neutrality view and see whether they can be put to use for Meinongians. This is the task of the present subsection.

A prominent variety of the ontological neutrality view is the *substitutional* interpretation of the quantifier. It goes back to Ruth Barcan Marcus and is explained as follows: Consider a propositional function "*A*" which contains "*x*" as a free variable. A *substitution instance* of "*A*" is a formula that results in the substitution of a *value of the free variable x* for the variable.[44] The substitutional interpretation of "$\exists x A$" goes: Some substitution instance of *A* is true; or: there is at least one value of "*x*" such that "*A*" is true. The substitutional interpretation of "$\forall x A$" goes: All substitution instances of "*A*" are true; or: for all values of "*x*", "*A*" is true. (Marcus, 1962: 252f.) According to Marcus, quantification, thus conceived, does not, *by itself*, involve any ontological commitment. Marcus writes:

> Quantification is tied to the notion of an open sentence and only incidentally to a particular choice of variables. It has to do with the sorting of propositional functions into those which are true in some substitution instances (at least one), and those which are true in all substitution instances. Quantification *need* not be bound to the subject-predicate form unless we choose it as the basic form of a sentence. If we choose as values of the variables the names of things, the names of classes, or the names of properties, then it is no metaphysical mystery that instantiation and quantification will be about things, properties, and classes. The *notion* of quantification, the process involved, like the operations of the propositional calculus, goes beyond the particular choice of basic sentence form. (Marcus, 1962: 253; emphasis in original text)

The important point to note here is that Marcus' interpretation of the quantifiers allows for the use of variables other than individual variables (i.e., variables that stand for *names*). As noted in Section 2 (Subsection 2.2, note 35), in standard logic, only individual variables are permitted, that is, variables in standard logic are to be replaced exclusively with names. It does not matter what kind of entities these names stand for. Standard logic allows for quantification over all kinds of things: not only individuals (in the usual sense) but also properties (conceived as

---

[44] Note that Marcus' use of "substitution instance" deviates from the more common Quinean use: In Quinean terms, it is *variables* that have substitution instances (not propositional functions), and the substitution instance of a variable is *an object* assigned to the variable, whereas in the context of substitutionalism, it is a linguistic item.

Platonist ideas), classes, propositions, numbers, names, and other linguistic entities. This is so because we can name all these entities. Consider, for instance: "Some properties are rarely exemplified." In standard notation, this may be rendered as: "∃x (Px ∧ Rx)" (where "P" stands for "is a property" and "R" stands for "is rarely exemplified"). A (probably true) substitution instance of "Rx" would be: "Wisdom is rarely exemplified." "Wisdom" is a singular term (a name) that stands for a universal. Therefore, the substitution of "wisdom" for "x" is wholly unproblematic, from the point of view of Quinean logic.

Marcus' point is not that we should interpret quantification substitutionally in order to allow for quantification over other things than individuals. Rather, her point is that we should interpret quantification substitutionally in order to allow for the substitution of linguistic expressions other than names for variables. Consider, for instance: "There is something that Ann and Bob have in common: They both like cold pizza." In order to render this sentence in standard logical notation, one would have to paraphrase it in terms of properties: "There is a property that both Ann and Bob exemplify . . . "; "∃x (Px ∧ Eax ∧ Ebx . . .)" (read: There is an x, such that x is a property, and Ann exemplifies x and Bob exemplifies x). Here, the variable x is to be replaced with a name for a property, for example, "the property of liking cold pizza". However, the substitutional interpretation of the quantifier à la Marcus allows for a straightforward rendering: "∃$Φ$ ($Φa$ ∧ $Φb$)" (read: There is a $Φ$, such that Ann $Φ$ and Bob $Φ$).[45] Here, the variable "$Φ$" is to be replaced not with a name but with the predicate "likes cold pizza".

As stated in the previous quotation, Marcus' interpretation of the quantifiers is independent of ontological considerations. Her point is simply that the very notion of quantification does not, by itself, force us to restrict ourselves to the exclusive use of nominal variables. The use of quantifiers requires variables. Variables are placeholders for linguistic expressions. For what kind of linguistic expressions? For any kind we like! Nothing in the concept of a variable prevents us from using variables for predicate expressions, propositions, adverbs, prepositions, or connectives.

Marcus' lucid observations about the nature of quantification and variables and her conclusion that the use of nonnominal variables should be admitted are surely correct. Moreover, as can be seen in the example of Ann and Bob, who both like cold pizza, the use of nonnominal variables may help to avoid unwanted ontological commitments. In this sense, one may say that quantification – substitutionally interpreted – is ontologically neutral. However, Marcus

---

[45] I use "$Φ$" as a variable for predicates, like "is red", "is a man", "knows how to swim". The proposal to use quantifiers with nonnominal variables was developed and given several applications by Arthur N. Prior (see Prior (1971)).

does not claim that quantifier statements *never* carry ontological commitments. As she puts it: "If we choose as values of the variables the names of things, the names of classes, or the names of properties, then it is no metaphysical mystery that instantiation and quantification will be about things, properties, and classes" (Marcus, 1962: 253). In other words, it is not the quantifier "∃x" that carries the ontological commitment but the nominal variables, that is, the variables that are placeholders for names. As soon as we connect the quantifier with a nominal variable, the quantification carries ontological commitment. Marcus' claim is not that quantifications per se are ontologically neutral but rather the much more cautious claim that it depends on the choice of variables whether a quantification carries ontological commitment. Consider, for instance, the following statement: "∃x (x is a fictitious entity)." Given that x is a nominal variable (to be replaced, for instance, with "Pegasus"), someone who accepts this statement as true is ontologically committed to fictitious objects, according to Marcus' substitutionalism.

Similar considerations can already be found more than ten years earlier in Peter Geach's critical discussion of Quine:

> Quine ... seems to take it for granted that if the predicate "red" stands for anything, then it stands for what the abstract name "redness" stands for ... Whatever "redness" may or may not stand for, the predicate "red" certainly stands for something. If A and B are both red, then there is something that they both are, and "red" stands for this.
>
> Quine thinks that if I say "A and B both are something, viz., red", this commits me to recognizing two sorts of entities: concrete entities like A and B, and abstract entities like what A and B are. His mistake is like the following one: "Jemima and Ahab, being cats, are the same animal. So there are two sorts of animals: concrete individual animals, like Jemima and Ahab; and abstract universal animals, like the Cat – the animal that Jemima and Ahab both are". The essential point here is that the phrase
> "the animal that Jemima and Ahab both are"
> so far from being a name of a third, abstract animal, is a logical predicate and not a name at all. (Geach, 1951: 132f.)

Geach's point is very similar in spirit to Marcus' insight: The (natural language) quantifier "something" does not necessarily involve *nominal* quantification. Although it may sound a bit odd as an English sentence, one can say: "There is something that Jemima and Ahab both are." The statement can be continued with " ... namely, a cat/red/hungry etc." But "a cat", "red", "hungry", and so on, are not names. In this case, the quantifier "something" is not tied to a variable that is a placeholder for a name.

In this sense, Geach as well as Marcus and Prior (see note 45) argue for an ontologically neutral interpretation of quantification, but neither of them denies that ontological commitment is carried by the use of nominal variables. Therefore, this kind of neutrality view – although extremely useful in certain contexts – cannot be applied to the topic discussed in the preceding subsection, where we considered only quantification with nominal variables. After all, Meinongianism is about the existence or nonexistence of *objects*. When Meinongians talk about nonexistent objects, they make use of nominal variables.

However, there are more radical varieties of the ontological neutrality view that are directly relevant to the topic under discussion. Some philosophers claim that utterances in the "object language" are ontologically neutral *tout court*. It is only at the level of *metalanguage* that we get involved in ontological commitments. In this context, an utterance in the object language is meant to be an utterance about nonlinguistic items, whereas an utterance in the metalanguage is an utterance about language (i.e., about linguistic items). Frank Jackson, for instance, puts this as follows:

> Consider the true sentence "Mr Pickwick is Dickens's most famous character". . . . "Mr Pickwick is Dickens's most famous character" does not force us to acknowledge the existence of Mr. Pickwick because "Mr Pickwick" in this sentence fails to denote, it is a name in form only. *If* we assented to "'Mr Pickwick' denotes Dickens's most famous character", then we would be admitting Mr Pickwick into our ontology, but it is, precisely, the latter sentence which we should not assent to. . . . In short, the crucial question is not what one assents to in the object language, but what one assents to in the metalanguage which explicitly states the semantical roles of the terms in the object language.
>
> In the case of general terms, true ontological seriousness is indicated by preparedness to express one's sentences in terms of the semantic relation of being true of or application. Thus, when we assent to "There are comic characters in Dickens", our assent is not to be granted ontological status unless we are prepared also to assent to "There are things which 'is a comic character in Dickens' applies to". (Jackson, 1980: 310)

If one appropriates Jackson's view on the meaning of "there is" in the object language and uses the quantifier as the logical symbol for "there is", this entails that the quantifier is ontologically neutral. Therefore, Jackson's version of the ontological neutrality view proves relevant to the topic under discussion.

Jackson's view is reminiscent of Rudolf Carnap's distinction between "internal" and "external" existence statements (Carnap, 1950). Basically, Carnap's idea is this: Both in everyday talk and in science, our use of general terms always happens within a particular "framework". If a speaker claims that there is a prime number bigger than 100, she presupposes the framework of numbers. If a speaker asks whether there is a mythical figure that is half-man and half-horse, he presupposes the framework of mythology, and so forth. Questions and statements of this kind are *internal* statements and questions. According to Carnap, internal statements and questions are, in principle, ontologically innocuous. They are not to be answered by philosophers but by mathematicians, literary theorists, or other specialists – depending on what kind of expertise a particular framework requires. The internal existence statement that there is a prime number bigger than 100 entails, trivially, the more general existence statement that there are numbers. This can also be regarded as an internal statement within the framework of numbers (though a trivial one).

However, Carnap (rightly) observes that ontologists do not think that questions like "Are there numbers?", "Are there mythical creatures?", and so on can be trivially answered on the basis of some kind of nonphilosophical expertise. Carnap concludes that, in ontology, these questions must be understood in a different way – namely, in an *external* way. When an ontologist asks, for instance, whether numbers exist, she does not presuppose the framework of numbers. Instead, it is the very presupposition of this framework that is at stake.

As Carnap sees it, external questions of this kind do not have a cognitive sense. If they are meaningful at all, they have to be understood as mere *pragmatic* questions, in the sense of: *Should* we accept the framework of numbers/mythical creatures, and so on? In other words, according to Carnap, external existence statements are to be understood as mere recommendations to make use of a certain framework. Such statements do not have any claim to truth. If they are neither understood in this pragmatic way nor in an internal sense, they are simply meaningless. One could say that Carnap, just like Jackson, considers the "object language" to be ontologically neutral.[46] Thus, Carnap's view on ontology also suggests an ontologically neutral interpretation of the quantifier.

3.3 Is *Außersein* a Third Mode of Being?

In the previous subsections of this section, two possible interpretations of the quantifier "$\exists x$" have been presented: the modes of being view and the ontological neutrality view. Which one of these is "the Meinongian" interpretation? The short answer is: There is no single Meinongian interpretation of the quantifier. Meinongianism is compatible with both the modes of being view and the neutrality view. Thus, it does not come as a surprise that there is no uniform position among Meinongians with regard to this issue.

Moreover, there is no uniform position among historians of Meinongianism with regard to the question of whether Meinong himself held the modes of being view or the neutrality view.[47] The truth is that Meinong struggled with this issue

---

[46] Recently, the Carnapian view on ontology has been revived by Amie Thomasson (see Thomasson (2015)). See also Subsection 5.3.

[47] The majority of commentators ascribes to Meinong the neutrality view; see Griffin (1977); Rapaport (1978): 155–157; Parsons (1980); Jacquette (1996); Grossmann (2001); Priest (2005): 106f.; Landini (2007). As will be shown, this interpretation must be based on ignorance of some of Meinong's later writings. Schubert Kalsi (1972: xxxvif., 1978: 7, and 1980: 116) and Perszyk

for decades, from the earliest presentation of object theory until the end of his life – although (of course) not in terms of the interpretation of "∃x",[48] but in terms of the interpretation of *Außersein*. His views changed over time. At the beginning, he tended toward the neutrality view; at the end, he opted for the modes of being view.

In order to get a complete picture of the development of Meinong's views about this issue, one has to take into account not only his more prominent early writings on the theory of objects, but also some later material, part of which was only published posthumously and is not yet available in an English translation. As mentioned *en passant* in Subsection 1.1, Meinong indeed distinguishes between various modes of being, namely, existence and subsistence. Objects like The Golden Mountain and The Round Square, however, have neither of these. They are, as Meinong calls it in one place, "beyond being and non-being". For this particular status, Meinong coined the term *Außersein* (Meinong, 1904/1960: §4). The objects that we are calling, in the present Element, *nonexistent* are, in Meinong's terms, *außerseiend*.[49] The question is: Is *Außersein* a third mode of being, over and above existence and subsistence? There is textual evidence that Meinong originally considered this option seriously, albeit reluctantly:

> it appears that the requirement that the Object have being (which was inferred from the being of a *Nichtseinsobjektiv*) makes sense only insofar as the being in question is neither existence nor subsistence – only insofar as a third order of being, if one may speak this way, is adjoined to existence and subsistence. This sort of being must belong, therefore, to every Object as such. ... The term *"Quasisein"* seemed to me for a while to be a completely suitable expression for this rather oddly constituted type of being. (Meinong, 1904/1960: §4)[50]

(1993) take at least some of these writings into account and – correctly – ascribe to Meinong the modes of being view. For an excellent discussion of this matter, see Perszyk (1993): note 5, p. 80f. and section 2.4. See also Marek (2022): section 5.3.1.

[48] Meinong did not make any use of formal languages. He was not educated in mathematical logic. Moreover, he had suffered from poor eyesight since he was a young man, and in his later years he was almost blind. He could take notice of philosophical literature only because his wife read it out loud to him; and he could write only because he used a typewriter (which was something extraordinary back then). (See Dölling (2001).) His handicap made it practically impossible for him to make use of logical notations à la Russell and Frege.

[49] The terms *Außersein* and *außerseiend* are difficult to translate. In standard contexts, the German *außer* may be used in the sense of "except" and "besides", among others. However, more pertinent in this context is its occurrence in the compound word *außerhalb* (outside). In the Chisholm edition (see the entry Meinong (1904/1960) in the list of references), *außerseiend* is translated (at least once) as "indifferent to being" (p. 86). This makes sense in this particular context. However, as a general translation, it would be unduly tendentious because it suggests an ontological neutrality view, which Meinong never wholeheartedly accepted and sometimes explicitly rejected, as will be pointed out.

[50] The translation is taken from the Chisholm edition; the quotation is to be found on p. 84 of this edition.

However, immediately following this passage, Meinong himself raises doubts about this interpretation:

> Can being which is in principle unopposed by non-being be called being at all? However much we are permitted in this connection to judge that there is a being which is neither existence nor subsistence, nowhere else do we find grounds for such a postulate. Must we not take thought to avoid it in our case also wherever it is possible? (Meinong, 1904/1960, English translation: 85)

In order to understand Meinong's worries, one has to take into account that *Außersein* is a status that does not only belong to nonexistent (and nonsubsistent) objects, but also to existent and subsistent objects. Thus, every object is *außerseiend*; there is no such thing as an object that lacks *Außersein*. There is no negative opposition to *Außersein*, whereas the established modes of being (existence and subsistence) have this negative opposition.

Of course, these considerations are far from ruling out definitely that *Außersein* is a third mode of being.[51] Meinong himself takes up the question again in his monograph *Über Annahmen* (*On Assumptions*) from 1910.[52] There, he fails to give a definite answer, although it becomes clear that he wishes to have an argument for the view that *Außersein* is not a third kind of being (Meinong, 1910/1968: §12, 78–80). In several later writings, however, Meinong explicitly declares that *Außersein* is indeed a third kind of being, over and above existence and subsistence.[53]

3.4 Neo-Meinongian and Other Contemporary Interpretations of "∃x"

Despite the almost universal occurrence of an existence predicate in neo-Meinongian logics, Meinongian logicians differ in their use of the quantifier "∃x". Some interpret it – as one might expect – as "ontologically neutral", that is, as not expressing existence;[54] others, however, use it as "ontologically loaded".[55]

---

[51] As Bertrand Russell already noted in his review of *Untersuchungen zur Gegenstandstheorie und Psychologie* (Russell (1905b): 532, note 2). See also Perszyk (1993): section 2.4.

[52] *Über Annahmen* appeared for the first time in 1902. However, the canonical version is the second, substantially revised, edition from 1910.

[53] See Meinong (1908/1978: 153f.; 1913/1978: 261; 1917/1968: §2; 1917–1918/1978: 358; 1921/1978: Zweiter Abschnitt, Hauptaufstellungen, section B, 21). Meinong (1908/1978) and (1913/1978) were only published posthumously in the *Alexius Meinong Gesamtausgabe, Ergänzungsband*; the page references are to this edition. The page reference to (1921/1978) is to the original edition from 1921 (which is also given in the reprint in the *Gesamtausgabe*).

[54] Rescher (1959): section III; Rapaport (1978): 165; Parsons (1980); Zalta (1983 and 1988); Paśniczek (1998): section 3.6.

[55] Routley (1980): chapter 1, §9; Lambert (1983): 105 and Lambert (1991); Priest (2005): 13f.; Berto (2013): section 7.6. Priest and Routley introduce an additional pair of quantifiers

Kit Fine defends an ontology of what he calls "arbitrary objects". Arbitrary objects are abstract objects akin to Meinongian incompletely determined nonexistent objects (at least in one important interpretation of Meinongian nonexistent objects):

> In addition to individual objects, there are arbitrary objects: in addition to individual numbers, arbitrary numbers; in addition to individual men, arbitrary men. With each arbitrary object is associated an appropriate range of individual objects, its values: with each arbitrary number, the range of individual numbers; with each arbitrary men, the range of individual men. An arbitrary object has those properties common to the individual objects in its range. So an arbitrary number is odd or even, an arbitrary man is mortal, since each individual number is odd or even, each individual man is mortal. On the other hand, an arbitrary number fails to be prime, an arbitrary man fails to be a philosopher, since some individual number is not prime, some individual man is not a philosopher. (Fine, 1983: 55)

Fine is aware that many philosophers would deny that there are such things as arbitrary objects. His reply is: It depends on how one interprets "there are". If one interprets it in an ontological sense, he would agree. However, he himself interprets it in an ontologically neutral way when he claims that "there are arbitrary objects" (Fine, 1983: 56f.).

In a similar spirit, Tim Crane argues that the use of the quantifier "$\exists x$" (or its natural-language equivalent "there is") does not entail any ontological commitment. Therefore, the claim that there are objects that do not exist is ontologically unproblematic and does not entail a distinction between "modes of being" in an ontologically relevant way (Crane, 2012: 425f. and 2013).[56]

In a recent paper, Nathanael Gan argues that Meinongianism in general is an *anti-realist* view, in that Meinongians "are not ontologically committed to the objects in question" (Gan, 2021: 53). The objection that Meinongianism involves "an unacceptably profligate ontology" (Gan, 2021: 54) is at least premature, if not wholly beside the point.[57] Obviously, the crucial question is how the "there are" in "there are nonexistent objects" is understood.

A neutrality view of quantification is also defended – for various reasons – in Routley, 1980; Lewis, 1990; Priest, 2005, and Paoletti, 2015. Others argue for

---

(in Priest's symbolism, "$\mathfrak{S}$", "$\mathfrak{A}$"), in addition to the familiar ones ("$\exists$", "$\forall$") – and in addition to an existence predicate. "$\mathfrak{S}$" and "$\mathfrak{A}$" stand for "some" and "all" and are to be interpreted as ontologically neutral quantifiers, while "$\exists$" and "$\forall$" are "existentially loaded". A similar solution is sketched in Rescher (1959): section IV; Berto (2013): 70f.

[56] According to Crane, there are true statements about nonexistent objects, although there are no nonexistent objects. This is possible because aboutness is not a real relation. Thus, Crane is not a Meinongian. Cf. Subsection 1.2.1, note 11.

[57] However, it seems that Gan himself is less than rock-solidly convinced of his anti-realist interpretation of Meinongianism. See note 6 on p. 54 of Gan (2021).

what one could call a "plurality view" of quantification, that is, that quantification can be used in various ways, both ontologically committing and noncommitting (see Linsky, 1972 and Hofweber, 2000).

By contrast, in so-called *Free Logics*, the quantifier is always interpreted as having "existential import" (see Lambert, 1983: 105; Lambert, 1991: 3). Free Logics are free from existence assumptions, both with respect to general and to singular terms. The latter kind of freedom (freedom of existence assumptions with respect to singular terms) distinguishes them from standard logics of the Quinean brand. In Quinean logic, it is simply assumed that singular terms that are substituted for individual variables are *denoting* singular terms. That is why, in Quinean logics, the principle of existential generalization (EG) holds unrestrictedly: $Fa \rightarrow \exists x Fx$. That is, in a formula "Fa", the "a" must be understood as a nonempty singular term. Free logicians, by contrast, feel that logical principles should hold independently of contingent matters of existence and denotation. Therefore, they reject (EG). As soon as (EG) is rejected, however, there is no need to interpret the quantifier "$\exists x$" in an ontologically neutral way.

Still others, for instance the neo-Meinongian logician Terence Parsons, remain impartial with respect to the interpretation of the quantifier.[58] Parsons even surmises (wrongly, in my view) that the issue might be merely terminological (Parsons, 1980: 10f.).

The neo-Meinongian logician Edward N. Zalta, however, explicitly holds a modes of being view. He takes the quantifier to express *being* (that is, "logical or metaphysical existence"), in contrast to the existence predicate "E!", which expresses "physical existence" (Zalta, 1988: 102f.).

A special case is Nino Cocchiarella. He distinguishes between various modes of existence (actual existence, past existence, future existence, merely possible existence) and proposes to introduce for each mode of existence an existential quantifier of its own. Alluding to Quine's famous slogan, he says "that *to be (of a given mode of being) is to be the value of a variable bound by a quantifier (comprehending that mode of being)*". (Cocchiarella, 1969: 42; emphasis in original text)

To sum up: Meinongianism is compatible with both the neutrality view and the modes of being view of the quantifier. Meinongians (including Meinong himself) do not have a uniform stance with regard to this question.[59]

---

[58] It seems that Dale Jacquette has a similar view. He avoids a clear commitment to either the modes of being or the neutrality interpretation of the quantifier. However, he notes that Meinongianism may be interpreted as ontologically sparse and nominalistic (Jacquette (1996): 10f., 166f.).

[59] This issue will be taken up again in Subsection 5.3.

3.5 Existential Generalization, Universal Instantiation, and the Predication Principle

Existential Generalization (EG), Universal Instantiation (UI), and the Predication Principle (PP) are logical principles that hold in Quinean logics without restriction:

(EG) $Fa \rightarrow \exists x Fx$

(UI) $\forall x Fx \rightarrow Fa$

(PP) $Fa \rightarrow \exists x(x = a)$

Are these principles acceptable for Meinongians? That depends on how the quantifiers are interpreted. If they are interpreted as ontologically neutral, all three principles are unproblematic from a Meinongian point of view. The same is true if the quantifiers are interpreted as expressing a mode of being other than existence, such that every object has this kind of being. (Cf. Subsection 3.3, on the debate about Meinong's notion of *Außersein*.)

Things are different, however, if "$\exists x$" is interpreted as expressing existence (or some other kind of being such that not every object has it). Consider EG first: If the quantifier is interpreted as "ontologically loaded", EG contradicts one of the Meinongian core principles, namely the principle of independence (IP) (see Subsection 1.1). Remember the paradox that arises from the statement "Pegasus is a flying horse" (Subsection 1.2.3). According to EG, this implies "$\exists x$ (x is a flying horse)," which seems to be false if the quantifier is taken to express existence. Consequently, neo-Meinongians who interpret the quantifier as expressing existence have to reject EG.[60] They can, however, accept the following revised version of EG:

(EG^R) $(Fa \wedge E!a) \rightarrow \exists x Fx$.
(Read: If a is F, and if a exists, then there is something that is F.)

Analogous reasoning holds for UI. If universal quantification is taken to be restricted to the domain of the existent, it is not acceptable for a Meinongian. Consider:

$\forall x$ (x is completely determined).

According to UI, this would imply, for instance: The Golden Mountain is completely determined. However, as we know (see Subsection 2.2), The Golden Mountain is not completely determined. Consequently, some neo-Meinongians

---

[60] See Routley (1980): 43; Lambert (1983): 106f.; Berto (2013): section 6.3.3.

reject UI (see Routley, 1980: 107; Lambert, 1983: 106f.). They may accept, however, a restricted version of it, namely:

(UI^R) $(\forall xFx \land E!a) \rightarrow Fa$.

(Read: If everything is F, and if a exists, then a is F.)

Now consider PP: In Quinean logic, PP is trivially true because there "$\exists x \ (x = a)$" is a logical truth, just like "$\forall x \ (x = x)$". This is because Quinean logic involves an existential presupposition with respect to singular terms. That is, it is presupposed that any individual constant that is used in a formula represents a *denoting* singular term. There is simply no provision for nondenoting (empty) singular terms. The rejection of this existential presupposition with respect to singular terms is the core of Free Logics (see the previous subsection). Neo-Meinongians who interpret the existential quantifier as expressing existence and the universal quantifier as restricted to the domain of existents (as, for instance, the Free Logician Karel Lambert does) have to reject "$\forall x \ (x = x)$", and they can no longer take "$\exists x \ (x = a)$" as a logical truth: "$\exists x \ (x = $ The Golden Mountain)," for instance, would be a falsehood. Consequently, neo-Meinongians who interpret the quantifier as expressing existence have to reject PP because it contradicts the principle of independence. They may only accept the following restricted version of PP:

(PP^R) $Fa \land E!a \rightarrow \exists x \ (x = a)$.

However, neo-Meinongians who interpret the quantifier as ontologically neutral may accept PP in its original version.

Finally, consider the following rendering of PP, which is possible in logics with an existence predicate "E!":

(PP') $Fa \rightarrow E!a$.

If the quantifier is interpreted as expressing existence, PP' and PP are equivalent. Consequently, PP' is to be rejected by neo-Meinongians of all kinds because it is in conflict with the principle of independence.

4 Meinongianism Extended and Refined

In Subsection 1.1, two basic principles of Meinongianism were presented: the characterization principle (CP: To every set of properties, there is a corresponding object, which has all and only the properties in the set) and the principle of independence (IP: An object's *so-being* is independent of its *being*). It was shown that these principles raise a number of logical problems. Among other things, they seem to violate the principle of excluded middle (PEM) and the principle of noncontradiction (PNC). Some Meinongian solutions to these problems were presented in Section 2.

Perhaps the most fundamental issue of Meinongianism is the distinction between "there is" and "exists". How this distinction can be understood in terms of quantifier logic was the topic of Section 3.

There are, however, at least two issues that still require further clarification: the problem of The Existent Golden Mountain and the paradox of simplicity. In what follows, it will be shown that Meinong's own extension and refinement of object theory provides solutions to both problems.

4.1 The Nuclear–Extranuclear Distinction

The distinction between nuclear and extranuclear properties first occurs in Meinong's writings in his monograph *Über Möglichkeit und Wahrscheinlichkeit* (1915/1972), §25. Meinong's starting point is the observation that nonexistent objects may be (and in most cases are) indeterminate with respect to many properties (see Subsection 2.2). Consider, for instance, the object The Blue. The Blue is neither round nor square, nor elliptical, and so on. It is indeterminate with respect to its shape, among many other things. In a similar vein, The Triangle is neither right-angled nor oblique-angled, neither equilateral nor scalene. Moreover, it is indeterminate with respect to its color, size, location, and so on.

Let's stay with the case of The Triangle: It has been observed that it is indeterminate with respect to its color. Neither the "The Triangle is blue" nor "The Triangle is red," and so on, are true. But what about the higher-order property of being indeterminate with respect to its color? Can't we say that The Triangle is determinate with respect to *this* property? After all, it seems to be an uncontested truth (within the framework of object theory) that The Triangle is indeterminate with respect to its color.

Meinong's answer is: Yes, being indeterminate with respect to its color does indeed belong to the properties of The Triangle. However, this property is not on a par with the property of having exactly three sides and the property of having exactly three angles. While the latter are *nuclear* properties of The Triangle, the former belongs to its *extranuclear* properties.[61]

Meinong gives two examples for nuclear properties (being red, being triangular) and two examples for extranuclear properties – being indeterminate with respect to this-and-this property and being simple (i.e., having exactly one

---

[61] Meinong (1915/1972): §25, 175–177. Meinong uses the terms "konstitutorisch" and "außerkonstitutorisch" (roughly, "constitutive" and "extra-constitutive") for this distinction. The (nowadays familiar) wording "nuclear" and "extranuclear" goes back to John N. Findlay (1963). The distinction itself goes back to Ernst Mally (see Subsection 1.3), as Meinong himself notes.

nuclear property). Moreover, Meinong makes it plain that an object's nuclear properties – and only these – constitute the object's "nature". It also becomes clear that the nuclear–extranuclear distinction entails an essential revision of the original version of Meinong's object theory: the comprehension principle (CP, see Subsection 1.1) becomes restricted to nuclear properties. The restricted version (CP^R) goes as follows:

(CP^R) To every set of *nuclear* properties, there is a corresponding object, either an existent or a nonexistent one, which has all the nuclear properties in the set and no other nuclear properties.

This restriction seems to set limits to what Meinong calls "freedom of assumption" (*Annahmefreiheit*): The principle of the unrestricted freedom of assumption is a correlate of CP. It says that we are free to assume (imagine, think of, …) any object we like, that we can "grasp", as it were, intentional objects on the basis of arbitrary sets of intended properties (i.e., those properties that are present to the mind in a particular act of presentation of an object), such that the grasped objects have the properties in question (cf. Meinong, 1915/1972: §37, p. 282). According to CP^R, however, we are confined to nuclear properties for our choice of intentional objects.

It is worth noting that nonexistent objects are incomplete with respect to their *nuclear* properties only. With respect to their extranuclear properties, they are as complete as any existent object. Moreover, impossible nonexistent objects (like The Round Square) have incompatible nuclear properties, but never incompatible extranuclear properties. The (seeming) conflict with PEM and PNC arises with respect to nuclear properties only.[62]

The nuclear–extranuclear distinction provides a solution to the paradox of simplicity (see Subsection 2.4). Consider the following structured presentation of the paradox:

1. The Blue has the property of being blue as its sole property. (According to CP.)
2. The Blue has the property of being blue. (1)
3. The Blue has the property of having exactly one property. (1)
4. The Blue has the property of being blue and the property of having exactly one property. (2, 3)
5. The Blue has at least two properties (namely, the property of being blue and the property of having exactly one property). (4; contradicts 3)

---

[62] Independently of the nuclear–extranuclear distinction, Meinongianism is compatible with PEM and PNC, as argued in Subsections 2.2 and 2.3.

The contradiction can be avoided in the following way: One has to take into account that being blue is a *nuclear* property, while the property of having exactly one property is an *extranuclear* property. In light of this, the propositions of the above deduction have to be reformulated as follows:

1'. The Blue has the property of being blue as its sole *nuclear* property. (According to CP.)
2'. The Blue has the *nuclear* property of being blue. (1)
3'. The Blue has *the extranuclear* property of having exactly one nuclear property. (1)
4'. The Blue has the nuclear property of being blue and the extranuclear property of having exactly one nuclear property. (2', 3')
5'. The Blue has exactly one nuclear and at least one extranuclear property. (4)

5' is not in conflict with any of the propositions 1'–4'. No contradiction arises. (Cf. Meinong, (1915/1972: §25), 175f.)

The nuclear–extranuclear distinction also allows for a straightforward solution to the problem of The Existent Golden Mountain and thus provides a powerful rejoinder to Russell's most serious objection (see Subsection 2.3). Consider a structured representation of the problem:

1. $\neg\exists x$ (x is golden $\wedge$ x is a mountain $\wedge$ x exists).
2. The Existent Golden Mountain is golden and a mountain and existent. (According to CP.)
3. The Existent Golden Mountain is existent. (2)
4. The Existent Golden Mountain exists. (3)
5. $\exists x$ (x is golden $\wedge$ x is a mountain $\wedge$ x exists) (namely, the Existent Golden Mountain). (2, 4; contradicts 1)

If existence is an extranuclear property and CP is restricted to nuclear properties only, then there is no such thing as The Existent Golden Mountain, that is, no object that has being a mountain, being golden, and being existent as its nuclear properties. That is, premise 2 in the above deduction is to be rejected. Thus, 3–5 cannot be derived, and no contradiction arises.

Surprisingly, Meinong does not take this straightforward path. He does not even mention existence as an example of an extranuclear property.[63] Instead, he infamously allows for the assumption of the object The Existent Golden Mountain and claims that there is a difference between existing and being existent. Meinong explains that being existent, but not existing, may belong

---

[63] For those neo-Meinongians who make use of the nuclear–extranuclear distinction, existence is one of the most important examples of an extranuclear property (see Subsection 5.4.1).

to an object's nature, the set of an object's determinations. Consequently, while we cannot assume The *Existing* Golden Mountain, we can indeed assume The *Existent* Golden Mountain. This move allows for an alternative solution of the Existent-Golden-Mountain problem. Let us disambiguate propositions 1–3 of the above deduction:

1'. $\neg \exists x$ (*x* has the nuclear property of being golden $\wedge$ *x* has the nuclear property of being a mountain $\wedge$ *x* has the *extranuclear* property of existing).
2'. The Existent Golden Mountain has the nuclear properties of being a mountain, of being golden and of being existent. (According to CP.)
3'. The Existent Golden Mountain has the nuclear property of being existent. (2')

From 3', however, we cannot derive

4'. The Existent Golden Mountain has the *extranuclear* property of existing.

Consequently, it cannot be derived that

5'. $\exists x$ (*x* has the nuclear property of being golden $\wedge$ *x* has the nuclear property of being a mountain $\wedge$ *x* has the extranuclear property of existing).

Therefore, no contradiction arises.

The crucial point is that the nuclear property of being existent does not entail the extranuclear property of existing. At first sight, it might seem (as Russell obviously suspected) that the distinction between existing and being existent is a desperate ad hoc maneuver in order to save object theory from inconsistency. But is it? After all, Meinong's restriction of CP to nuclear properties suffices to meet Russell's challenge (see Subsection 2.3). Either Meinong simply did not see this easy solution to the problem of The Existent Golden Mountain and therefore contrived the doctrine of nuclear counterparts of extranuclear properties, or he had an independent reason for doing so. In the following subsection, it will be argued that the latter is the case.

4.2 A Functional Explanation of the Nuclear–Extranuclear Distinction

As has been shown, the nuclear–extranuclear distinction may be a valuable tool for saving object theory from inconsistencies. Its main problem is that it is not easy to understand. It is not at all clear from the outset which properties are supposed to be nuclear and which are supposed to be extranuclear. There is no obvious criterion for sorting properties neatly into nuclear and extranuclear ones. Meinong's explanations are sometimes more confusing than clarifying.

Since the nuclear–extranuclear distinction led to a restriction of CP, it concerns the very foundation of object theory. Not least for this reason, it would be highly desirable to have a clear conception of it. In what follows, I will propose an unorthodox explanation, suggested by Meinong himself in the following passages:

> The conception of an 'A that is not yet determined with respect to its B-determination' doubtlessly could be constructed; in this case, however, the feature 'B-determination' would have, in its turn, nuclear character, such that the validity of the principle of excluded middle would remain in force in the domain of the extranuclear. (Meinong, 1915/1972: 177f.; my translation)

> It must remain unexamined here on what it may depend whether a given determination *functions*, as it were, as a nuclear or as an extranuclear one . . .. (Meinong, 1915/1972: 190; my translation; my emphasis)

These two passages strongly suggest that the nuclear–extranuclear distinction is not an absolute distinction among properties, that is, properties are not divided into two classes – nuclear and extranuclear – such that each property falls under exactly one of the two concepts. Rather, the nuclear–extranuclear distinction is a *functional* distinction. Instead of saying that a given property P *is* nuclear (or extranuclear), it would be better to say that, in a given context, P *functions* as a nuclear (or extranuclear) property, respectively.

To say that, in a given context, a property functions as a nuclear one is to say that it belongs to the object's nature, that it is used to define the object's essential properties. The property of being indeterminate with respect to some determination B is, in most circumstances, a typical example of an extranuclear property. It is an extranuclear property of The Blue that it is indeterminate with respect to being triangular. It is an extranuclear property of The Triangle that is indeterminate with respect to being blue; and so on. However, CP allows us to assume an object like The-Triangle-that-Is-Indeterminate-with-Respect-to-Being-Blue. In this case, the indeterminacy with respect to being blue belongs to the nature of the object in question and thus functions as a nuclear property. Similarly for existence: When we say of The Golden Mountain that it does not exist, we deny an extranuclear property of The Golden Mountain. We may, however, assume The Existent Golden Mountain, and in this case, existence (or being existent) functions as a nuclear property.

Unrestricted freedom of assumption is saved in the sense that we may assume at whim, for arbitrary Fs, an existent F, a completely determined F, and so forth. However, what we cannot do is make an arbitrary F exist or being completely determined. The Existent Golden Mountain still does not exist; The Completely Determined Blue is still an incomplete object; and so forth.

Remember the psychological origin of Meinong's object theory: the problem of intentionality (see Subsection 1.2.1). The first and foremost purpose of assuming nonexistent objects was to provide an intentional object for every mental act (imagination, thought, desire, etc.). If one takes this into account, the functional explanation of the nuclear–extranuclear distinction no longer seems ad hoc, but makes very good sense. For we may think not only of a golden mountain, but also of an existent golden mountain, not only of a triangle, but also of a completely determined triangle. That is, the content of our thoughts may contain existence and completeness along with being golden, being a mountain, and so on. However, the assumption of an existent golden mountain does not bring a golden mountain into existence. Merely adding the determination of completeness to a finite number of nuclear properties does not turn an incomplete object into a complete one (Meinong, 1915/1972: §37).

Thus, Meinong himself provides an explanation of the nuclear–extranuclear distinction. According to this explanation, each property that may function as an extranuclear property in one context may function as a nuclear property in another context. A property functions as a nuclear property of an object if, and only if, it is an element of the set that constitutes the object's essence. In principle, each property may be included in such an essence-constituting set.

The nuclear–extranuclear distinction is used by a number of neo-Meinongians. Others make use of an alternative distinction (the modes-of-predication distinction) instead of the nuclear–extranuclear distinction. We will come back to both distinctions in Subsection 5.4. In Subsection 5.4.4, it will be argued that the nuclear–extranuclear distinction, rightly conceived, is functionally equivalent to the modes-of-predication distinction.

4.3 Auxiliary Objects and Implexive Being

In *Über Möglichkeit und Wahrscheinlichkeit* (Meinong, 1915/1972), Meinong introduces several related concepts that give the whole theory of objects a completely new turn: auxiliary object (*Hilfsgegenstand*), target object (*Zielgegenstand*), and implexive being (*implexives Sein*).

Meinong argues that incomplete objects play an important epistemic role. In ordinary circumstances, we are intentionally directed toward existent (and thus completely determined) objects. In other words, in standard circumstances, our "target objects" are complete objects. However, our limited cognitive capacities do not allow us to fully comprehend (*erfassen*) a completely determined object. We are not able to comprehend the totality of the infinitely many features of a completely determined object. Rather, Meinong claims, we comprehend a complete object by means of an incomplete object. For instance, we may have an existent billiard ball as our target object. We may comprehend this complete object via the auxiliary object The Ball, that is, an object that has being a ball as its only nuclear property. In this case, The Ball is our direct intentional object, though the cognitive act ultimately aims at an existent billiard ball (Meinong, 1915/1972: §29).

Meinong struggles with the question of how exactly target objects and auxiliary objects are related to each other. First, he considers and rejects the idea that auxiliary objects are *parts* of target objects (in the usual sense of "part"). He – rightly – points out that the relation of The Ball to an existent billiard ball is clearly distinct from the relation of, for instance, a knife's handle and blade to the knife as a whole. However, Meinong considers the relation between a target object and its auxiliary objects as something analogous to the part–whole relation. In order to avoid confusion with the standard conception of a part, he introduces the term "implecting" (*implektieren*):

> I try to prevent the danger of taking similar things for identical through a particular designation, by saying of "the ball" [the auxiliary object] that it is "implected" in my friend's billiard ball, and by designating the latter ball as an "implectant" [*Implektant*] of the former. An incomplete object is implected in all those complete objects which one can think of as developing from it [the incomplete object], as it were. (Meinong 1915/1972: §29; my translation)

The auxiliary object The Ball has implexive being in all existent balls, including the particular billiard ball on a particular billiard table (Meinong 1915/1972: §29).

Meinong's discussion of the relation between incomplete auxiliary and complete target objects is reminiscent of Plato's struggle with the relation between (universal) "ideas" and particulars in the dialogue *Parmenides*. Implexive being seems to be a relation between universals and particulars, the relation between types and tokens. "The Ball is implected, among many other things, in the red billiard ball on my friend's table" seems to be another way of saying "The type The Ball is *instantiated*, among many other things, in the red billiard ball on my friend's table."

In the light of these considerations, Meinong's nonexistent objects seem to be abstract, ideal universal objects that can be instantiated in particulars. Thus, they would be objects that cannot have spatial properties such as being round. This would be a radical shift from the original version of object theory, according to which The Ball is a concrete object that *is* round, just in the same sense as the particular billiard ball on the friend's table. Meinong was perhaps not fully aware of this shift with all its far-reaching consequences while writing *Über Möglichkeit und Wahrscheinlichkeit*.[64] But there is evidence that he later became aware of it. In a sketchy note on *Über Möglichkeit und Wahrscheinlichkeit*, Meinong writes:

---

[64] In another passage of §29 of Meinong (1915/1972), Meinong points out that an auxiliary object may be implected not only in a complete and existent object, but also in an incomplete object. For instance, The Ball is implected in The Red Ball. The Red Ball is implected in The Red Wooden Ball, etc. But the relation between The Red Ball and The Ball is not instantiation, but rather

Incomplete objects underlie such early conceptions as the Platonic theory of ideas. Ideas are nothing but incomplete objects, to which one has erroneously attributed common being, even existence, instead of implexive being. . . .

[A]n object that is implected in another object is auxiliary object for the comprehension of the implectant . . . . Therefore, incomplete objects function as universals . . . . (Meinong, 1915/1972: 739f.; my translation.)[65]

However, this has a consequence that Meinong was obviously not aware of: If incomplete objects are ideal objects, they have – according to Meinong's original theory – a kind of being, namely subsistence (see Subsection 1.1), that is, they are not merely *außerseiend*. For philosophers who do not distinguish (like Meinong) between existence and subsistence, they are not nonexistent. They exist in the very same sense as numbers, properties, theories, institutions, laws, works of music and literature, and other ideal objects. Thus, according to this interpretation of the mature version of Meinong's object theory, the category of the nonexistent is empty. There is no longer any need for Meinong's concept of mere *Außersein*. It seems as if object theory was transformed from a theory of nonexistent objects into a sophisticated version of Platonism – or at least it came very close to such a transformation.

5 Neo-Meinongianism

5.1 Varieties of neo-Meinongianism

One of the aims of this section is to provide an overview of varieties of Meinongianism in contemporary philosophy,[66] a sort of roadmap that should help one orient oneself in a rather multifarious, complex, and sometimes confusing domain. This is not an easy task, for various reasons.

The first difficulty is that it is not entirely clear from the outset what belongs to the extension of the concept of neo-Meinongianism. In Subsection 1.1, I declared that I use the term "Meinongianism" for theories that include principle M, some version of CP, and IP, and that I use the term "neo-Meinongianism" in a loose sense – as a collective term for contemporary Meinongian philosophers, as well

---

something that one might call "inclusion". This may count as evidence against the Platonist interpretation of Meinong's theory of implexion. However, when reading Meinong, one should always keep in mind that the theory of objects was "work in progress" for Meinong until his death. *Über Möglichkeit und Wahrscheinlichkeit* was not his last word on it. See the quotations that follow in this subsection.

[65] This passage does not belong to the original version of *Über Möglichkeit und Wahrscheinlichkeit*, but to additional comments that Meinong wrote after 1915. They were only published posthumously in the *Gesamtausgabe* volume from 1972. The page reference is to this volume.

[66] I take the liberty to use "contemporary philosophy" in the present context in a rather wide sense, including everything from the 1950s onward.

as for those who, for one reason or another, are not Meinongians in the sense explicated in this Element, but who consider themselves to be Meinongians or are usually classified as Meinongians.

The second difficulty is that neo-Meinongian theories can be compared and classified along various coordinates, some of which run diagonal to each other. One can distinguish, for instance, "concrete neo-Meinongianism" from "abstract neo-Meinongianism", and "ontologically committing neo-Meinongianism" from "ontologically neutral neo-Meinongianism". Both concrete neo-Meinongianism and abstract neo-Meinongianism may be either ontologically committing or ontologically neutral.

The third difficulty is due to the limitation of space. Most (if not all) of the theories considered in what follows would deserve an extensive treatment, a detailed presentation and discussion, which would require several times the length of this Element. However, the limitation of space is not necessarily a disadvantage. After all, the aim of this Element is to provide a concise and comprehensible survey of the field, not an encyclopedic resource. Simplification will be unavoidable – hopefully simplification without distortion. Those readers who would like to dig deeper into some of the issues will find ample bibliographical references.

5.2 Concrete versus Abstract neo-Meinongianism

Borrowing a term from Fred Kroon, I start by distinguishing between two rather broad categories of Meinongianism, namely "concrete neo-Meinongianism" and "abstract neo-Meinongianism".[67] Concrete neo-Meinongianism is the view that Meinongian objects like The Golden Mountain, The Round Square, or The Blue are concrete objects. Abstract neo-Meinongianism is the view that all Meinongian objects are abstract objects.[68]

According to concrete neo-Meinongianism, The Golden Mountain is a concrete, spatio-temporal object. It has the properties of being golden and of being a mountain, in the ordinary sense of these expressions. The Golden Mountain is a mountain in the same sense in which Mount Everest is a mountain. It is golden in the same sense in which the Winged Victory statue on the top of the Victoria Memorial in London is golden.

By contrast, according to abstract neo-Meinongianism, The Golden Mountain is neither golden nor a mountain. It cannot have these features because it is an

---

[67] See Kroon (1996). To be exact, I borrow from Kroon the term "concrete Meinongianism". Instead of "abstract Meinongianism", Kroon uses the term "abstract objectualist view" (Kroon (1996): 163).

[68] The distinction is not exhaustive. There are Meinongians who are simply silent about the nature of nonexistent objects (see Lambert (1983)).

abstract object. As such, it is not spatio-temporally extended and located, and not perceivable by the senses and accessible to empirical investigation.

As shown in the previous sections, Meinong himself started out as a concrete Meinongian and ultimately ended up as an abstract Meinongian. The very same divide runs through neo-Meinongianism. The following philosophers belong to the camp of concrete neo-Meinongianism: Roderick M. Chisholm (1972), Terence Parsons (1980), Richard Routley (1980), Karel Lambert (1983), Dale Jacquette (1996), Jacek Paśniczek (1998), Graham Priest (2005), and Francesco Berto (2013).[69] Abstract neo-Meinongians include Nicholas Rescher (1959 and 1968),[70] Hector-Neri Castañeda (1972), Kit Fine (1983), Edward N. Zalta (1983 and 1988), Kenneth J. Perszyk (1993), Alberto Voltolini (2006), and probably also William J. Rapaport (1978, 1981, and 1985).

The camp of abstract neo-Meinongians can be further divided into those who consider Meinongian objects as universals, more precisely as Platonic *types* or *kinds*, and those who identify them with *sets of properties*.[71] In what follows, I will refer to the former as "the universalists" and to the latter as "the settists". Universalists are Zalta and Voltolini. A "settist" is Castañeda and probably Rapaport.[72]

A special case is Kenneth J. Perszyk. The core thesis of his book is that Meinong's "nonexistent objects" are to be interpreted as sets of properties, a claim that is repeated over and over again. However, at some point, it turns out that Perszyk actually interprets sets of properties as universals (Perszyk, 1993: 104–126 and note 22 on p. 144). So, despite his "settist" wording, he should be classified as a universalist.[73]

The difference between universalist and settist neo-Meinongianism can easily be overlooked because sets of properties play a crucial role in universalist

---

[69] I count as "concrete neo-Meinongians" all those who attribute properties to nonexistent objects that entail spatial localization, in the spirit of Meinong's theory of objects from 1904.

[70] Rescher explicitly commits himself to nonexistent objects, but he does not say much about their nature. I put him in the abstract camp because he refers to nonexistent objects as "purely conceptual objects" (Rescher (1959): 171–174), and because of the following remark: "A satisfactory formal analysis of the concept of existence can be provided in terms of the thesis that nonexistent objects can have no nontrivial qualitative properties (i.e., no such properties not possessed by everything)" (Ibid.: 180; similarly, Rescher (1968): 144–148.) I take it for granted that every concrete object has some nontrivial qualitative property.

[71] This distinction is also drawn in Voltolini (2006): 16f.

[72] Rapaport is not explicit about this matter, but he repeatedly (and in an approving manner) refers to the explicit "settist" Castañeda.

[73] Perszyk presents his version of neo-Meinongianism not as his own view but as an interpretation of Meinong. As Perszyk admits, the textual evidence in favor of the "settist" interpretation, taken literally, is rather thin. However, Perszyk correctly observes that there is good textual evidence for the universalist interpretation, and it is actually this evidence that he takes to corroborate his interpretation.

neo-Meinongianism too. After all, the pivotal principle of Meinongianism, CP, says that *to every set of properties*, there is a corresponding object which has (in some yet to be clarified sense of "has") the properties in the set. Nevertheless, the distinction is ontologically significant. A set of properties is something substantially different from an object that "has" the properties in the set. This is evident for concrete objects: Mount Everest is not a set of properties that includes the property of being a mountain, but it *is* a mountain (or exemplifies the property of being a mountain). A set of properties is an abstract object, a mountain is a concrete object.

In light of universalist neo-Meinongianism, however, Meinongian objects are just as abstract as sets. But there is a distinction. According to the universalist conception, Meinongian objects can be *instantiated* in concrete objects (after all, this is what makes them universals). Sets, however, are not the kind of abstract objects that can be instantiated.

One may question whether settist Meinongianism is really a variety of Meinongianism in the first place. After all, there are probably people out there who accept that there are sets of properties without thinking of themselves as Meinongians. Given that one accepts both properties and sets in one's ontology, there is no need to assume that some sets of properties are nonexistent objects. The set that contains the properties of being a mountain and being golden seems to be no less existent than the set that contains the properties of being a mountain and being rocky. However, Hector-Neri Castañeda, the main proponent of settist Meinongianism, explicitly declares himself to be a Meinongian, and rightly so, because he considers some sets of properties as nonexistent objects (Castañeda, 1972).

5.3 Committing versus Noncommitting neo-Meinongianism

In Section 3, we saw that "there is" in "There are objects that do not exist," as well as the quantifier "$\exists x$", is ambiguous in the sense that it can be read in an ontologically neutral and in an ontologically committing way. Moreover, it has been pointed out that interpreters of Meinong disagree on whether Meinong intended his theory of objects as committing or noncommitting.

It is not surprising that the same kind of disagreement occurs within neo-Meinongianism.[74] The following neo-Meinongians explicitly claim ontological neutrality for statements that seem to involve reference to nonexistent objects: Rapaport (1978): 155–158; Routley (1980): in particular chapter 1, §3; Fine (1983): 56f.; Paśniczek (1998): section 3.6; Priest (2005): in particular, vii, sections

---

[74] This is also noted in Eklund (2006): 328.

1.3 and 1.4.[75] Others either more or less explicitly accept an ontological commitment to nonexistent objects, or at least their writings provide some evidence for the commitment view and no evidence to the contrary: Rescher (1959: 171–174); Cocchiarella (1969): 34f.; Parsons (1980); Lambert (1983);[76] Zalta (1988: 102f.); Perszyk (1993: in particular, 11f.); Jacquette (1996): part one, chapter IV.

I agree with Perszyk's comment on the neutrality view:

> If Meinong or Routley or any other nonexistent-object theorist has moved out of the ontological game entirely, I cannot imagine what all the fuss over nonexistents has been about; but at the same time, I feel as if whatever feeble grasp I once had of the import of the claim that there are nonexistent objects has now slipped away. Meinongians quantify over nonexistent objects, yet some, e.g. Routley, insist that this does not involve *ontological* commitment. But if this involves no ontological commitment whatsoever, some of us would like to know more about this commitment to a something which is not a nothing but does not have being in any sense. . . . I would have thought that one is ontologically committed to whatever is within the domain of one's quantifiers, if they are interpreted objectually. If the claim that there are nonexistent objects is not metaphysical or ontological in at least this sense, then I am not sure that I understand it at all. (Perszyk, 1993: 11f.)

It has become fashionable in contemporary philosophy to make all sorts of claims and in the same breath to reject any ontological commitments that seem to be entailed by them. (Recently, this often goes under the flag of "fictionalism".[77]) Though I do not wish to deny that this may be an adequate approach for the analysis of some kinds of discourse, it seems to me that it is now used in an inflationary way, as a one-size-fits-all solution to get rid of all sorts of ontological commitments. In *philosophical* discourse, in particular, one should strive to say what one means and to mean what one says. Or, to borrow a formulation from John L. Austin: "It is better, perhaps, to stick to the old saying that our word is our bond" (Austin, 1979: 236).[78]

---

[75] See also Hofweber (2000). Hofweber clearly opts for the ontological neutrality view, but it is not clear to me whether he is to be classified as a Meinongian.

[76] Karel Lambert is one of the most prominent proponents of so-called Free Logic. Free Logic differs from standard logic in that it allows for the use of empty singular terms (in the sense of singular terms that do not denote anything existent). (See Subsection 3.4.) There are various versions of Free Logic: According to so-called negative Free Logics, all sentences that contain empty singular terms are false. Negative Free Logicians need not commit themselves to a Meinongian ontology. According to "positive Free Logics", however, some sentences with empty singular terms are true. Lambert defends a positive Free Logic and argues that this requires that the empty singular terms in question must denote *something*, an object. I take this as an avowal to a committing neo-Meinongianism (Lambert (1983); this book also provides an excellent introduction into Free Logics).

[77] For an introduction to fictionalism, see Eklund (2019).

[78] The quotation is taken from Austin's discussion of so-called performative utterances – a context that is very distinct from the present one.

5.4 Characterizing Properties and Predicates: The Perennial Problem Reconsidered

As shown in Subsection 2.3, the original version of Meinongianism threatens to contradict the principle of noncontradiction, because it seems to entail that there is not only The Golden Mountain but also The *Existent* Golden Mountain, which is both existent and nonexistent. In what follows, I will refer to this as "the paradox of The Existent Golden Mountain". However, there is another problem with the original version of Meinongianism, which has not been explicitly mentioned yet: According to the original version of Meinongianism, The Golden Mountain literally *is* golden and a mountain. But it seems reasonable to assume that an object that has properties like being golden and being a mountain can be perceived by the senses. In other words, properties like being golden and being a mountain (among many others) seem to be perceivability-entailing. But, as a matter of fact (a fact that is not questioned by any Meinongian), The Golden Mountain (like any other nonexistent object) cannot be perceived by the senses. Therefore, according to the original version of Meinongianism, it must be denied that there are any properties that are perceivability-entailing. This seems to be in conflict with our very understanding of properties like being golden and being a mountain. I refer to this as the problem of nonperceivability.

Any serious neo-Meinongian theory has to propose solutions both to the paradox of The Existent Golden Mountain and the problem of nonperceivability. Neo-Meinongian theories can be divided not only into concrete and abstract, or committing and noncommitting theories, but also with respect to how they try to resolve these problems.

It has been shown in Section 4 that Meinong himself proposed a solution to the paradox of The Existent Golden Mountain, namely the distinction between nuclear and extranuclear properties. Some neo-Meinongians have adopted this distinction (Parsons, 1980; Routley, 1980; Lambert, 1983; Jacquette, 1996). Others opt for an alternative solution, namely the modes-of-predication distinction (Castañeda, 1972; Rapaport, 1981; Zalta 1983 and 1988; Perszyk, 1993). Yet another solution is suggested by so-called Modal Meinongians (Priest, 2005 and 2008; Berto, 2013). I call their proposal "the other worlds strategy". Neo-Meinongians can hence be divided into three camps: advocates of the nuclear–extranuclear distinction, advocates of the modes-of-predication distinction, and advocates of the other worlds strategy.

All of the previously mentioned abstract neo-Meinongians (both the universalist and the settist) accept some kind of modes-of-predication distinction. None of them opt for the nuclear–extranuclear distinction. This is no coincidence. If the nuclear-extranuclear distinction is understood in the familiar way,

The Golden Mountain, for instance, literally *is* a mountain, in the usual sense. But abstract objects cannot be mountains. The nuclear–extranuclear distinction could be an option for abstract neo-Meinongians, however, if it is interpreted in the functional sense (see Subsection 4.2). However, if it is interpreted in this sense, it becomes functionally equivalent to the modes-of-predication distinction, as will be shown in Subsection 5.4.4. Concrete neo-Meinongians either opt for the nuclear–extranuclear distinction or for the other worlds strategy. In what follows, all three suggestions will be explained and discussed.

5.4.1 Nuclear and Extranuclear Properties and Predicates

In Section 4, I suggested (based on Meinong's own writings) a functional conception of the nuclear–extranuclear distinction. However, none of the neo-Meinongian advocates of this distinction interprets it in the functional way; and all of them seem to have overlooked that Meinong himself suggested a functional interpretation.[79]

According to these neo-Meinongians, there are two sorts of properties or predicates,[80] namely nuclear ones and extranuclear ones. Intuitively, nuclear properties are those that constitute the object's "essence"; extranuclear properties are not essence constituting.

One of the main problems of this solution is that none of its advocates provides a definition of, or a satisfactory criterion for, the nuclear–extranuclear distinction.[81] Basically, they rely on more or less intuitive examples. Parsons, for instance, distinguishes between the following kinds of extranuclear predicates:

> ontological predicates, e.g., "exists", "is fictitious" ... ;
> modal predicates, e.g., "is possible", "is impossible" ... ;
> intentional predicates, e.g., "is worshipped", "is thought about" ... ;
> technical predicates, e.g., "is completely determined", "is incomplete" ...
>   (Parsons, 1980: 22f.)

However, neo-Meinongians differ in their intuitive classifications. In contrast to Parsons, Jacquette considers intentional predicates to be extranuclear (Jacquette, 1996: 50). Who is right? There is no criterion to decide. This is unfortunate for the theory. In light of the functional interpretation of the nuclear–extranuclear distinction, this conundrum is easily resolved: Intentional predicates (just as

---

[79] However, a functional interpretation of Meinong is suggested in Perszyk (1993): 247, and in Jorgensen (2002): see p. 99 in particular.

[80] Neo-Meinongians often talk of nuclear and extranuclear *predicates* rather than of nuclear and extranuclear properties. In what follows, I will move back and forth between these two ways of speaking, just as Routley and Parsons do.

[81] For a discussion of several explanations and criteria that were proposed, see Reicher (2005).

predicates of any other sort) may function both as nuclear and as extranuclear ones. For instance, in "The Round Square was thought about by Meinong," "was thought about" functions as an extranuclear predicate. By contrast, in "Sherlock Holmes was thought about by his friend Watson," the same predicate functions as a nuclear one.

From the point of view of formal logic, the distinction between nuclear and extranuclear predicates requires further amendments of the formal language and the introduction of new principles. Parsons uses p_1, p_2, ... as nuclear predicate constants, q_1, q_2, ... as nuclear predicate variables, P_1, P_2, ... as extranuclear predicate constants, and Q_1, Q_2, ... as extranuclear predicate variables (Parsons, 1980: 64). Jacquette writes nuclear predicates as F, G, ..., and extranuclear ones as F!, G!, ... (Jacquette, 1996: 20f.). Using Parsons's symbolism, some important Meinongian principles can be represented as follows:

$\forall q \, \exists x (\neg E!x \wedge qx)$.
(Read: For every nuclear predicate q, there is a nonexistent x, such that x is q.)

$\forall q \, \exists x (\neg E!x \wedge qx \wedge \overline{q}x)$.
(Read: For every nuclear predicate q, there is a nonexistent x, such that x is both q and non-q.)

$\forall q \, \exists x ((\neg E!x \wedge \neg(qx \vee \overline{q}x)$.
(Read: For every nuclear predicate q, there is a nonexistent x, such that neither x is q nor x is non-q.)

Does the nuclear–extranuclear distinction resolve the paradox of The Existent Golden Mountain and the problem of nonperceivability? In the simple version presented in Subsection 4.1 (and this is the one that is under discussion here), it does not resolve the problem of nonperceivability: Many nuclear properties seem to be perceivability-entailing, but no nonexistent object is perceivable.

As to the paradox of The Existent Golden Mountain, the nuclear–extranuclear distinction provides the resources for a solution, namely: Since the property of being existent or existing (I use these terms as synonyms here) is classified as an extranuclear property, being existent cannot belong to an object's essence. Therefore, CP must be restricted to nuclear properties. Consequently, the answer to Russell must be that Meinongianism does not entail that there is The Existent Golden Mountain. In general, there is no nonexistent object that has being existent among its nuclear properties. Thus, the contradiction cannot arise.

This solution works, but it may be objected that the restriction of CP to nuclear properties considerably weakens the explanatory force of Meinongianism. Remember that Meinongianism is supposed to provide the foundation for a theory of intentionality, a theory of fictional objects, and a solution for negative singular existence statements, among other things. Now imagine a fictional story according to which people worship a golden mountain that does not exist. If CP is restricted to nuclear properties, and if being worshipped and being existent are extranuclear, there is no Meinongian object corresponding to the description "the nonexistent worshipped golden mountain". Thus, it seems, a lot of (actual and possible) fictitious objects would fall out of the scope of Meinongianism, which would be unfortunate.

Following Meinong, Parsons proposes a further refinement of the nuclear–extranuclear distinction to avoid this result: He suggests that, for every extranuclear property, there is a *nuclear counterpart* (Parsons, 1980: 42–44, 155). Thus, there is not only the *extranuclear* property of being existent, but also the *nuclear* property of being existent. Accordingly, the reply to the paradox of The Existent Golden Mountain is: The Existent Golden Mountain does have the nuclear property of being existent, but it lacks the extranuclear property of being existent. However, Parsons does not assume that, for every nuclear property, there is an extranuclear counterpart. Thus, although there is a nuclear counterpart of the extranuclear property of being existent, there is no extranuclear counterpart of the nuclear property of being a mountain, according to Parsons. So, Parsons's refined version of the nuclear–extranuclear distinction provides an elegant solution for the paradox of The Existent Golden Mountain due to the assumption of nuclear counterparts of extranuclear properties. However, this refined version still does not resolve the problem of nonperceivability.

5.4.2 Modes of Predication

The modes-of-predication distinction comes in several wordings: "consubstantiation"/"co-actuality" versus "composition"/"constitution" (Castañeda, 1972); "exemplifying" versus "being constituted by" (Rapaport, 1981); "encoding" versus "exemplification" (Zalta, 1983 and 1988); "generic" versus "classical readings of predicates" (Fine, 1984); "exemplification" versus "having as a constituent" (Perszyk, 1993). This distinction (just as the nuclear–extranuclear distinction) also goes back to Ernst Mally.[82]

To explain the distinction in Zalta's terminology: Every property may be either encoded or exemplified. The properties that are encoded by a nonexistent object are those that constitute the object's nature (in terms of the nuclear–extranuclear distinction: its nuclear properties). The properties of a nonexistent object that do not belong to the object's nature (in terms of the nuclear–extranuclear distinction: its extranuclear properties) are exemplified by the object. The object The Blue, for instance, encodes the property of being blue but exemplifies the property of being simple.

---

[82] See Mally (1912). For a detailed study of Mally, see Linsky (2014).

Note that all of the previously mentioned versions of the modes-of-predication distinction entail an ontological commitment to Platonic properties (if their wording is taken at face value), since all of them are explained as a distinction between two distinct relations between individuals and properties.[83] In this regard, they are on a par with the nuclear–extranuclear distinction, which – since it is a distinction of kinds of properties in the first place – trivially entails a Platonic ontology. But the modes-of-predication distinction at least avoids the *doubling* of the Platonic realm of properties. All that needs to be assumed, in addition to the standard Platonic metaphysical picture, is a second relation between individuals and properties in addition to the familiar relation of exemplification – namely, the relation of encoding.

More importantly, however, modes-of-predication theories even can avoid any commitment to Platonic properties and relations. For the modes-of-predication distinction can be expressed simply by two distinct copulas that join singular terms and general terms, instead of singular terms and names of properties (see Subsection 3.2). In what follows, I will stick to this simple and ontologically parsimonious interpretation, and I will use the following wording: The Golden Mountain *is determined as* being a mountain. Mount Everest *is* a mountain. The Existent Golden Mountain *is determined as* being existent. Mount Everest *is* existent. The Blue *is determined as* being blue, but *is* indeterminate with respect to its shape.

It is easy to see how the modes-of-predication distinction helps to resolve the paradox of The Existent Golden Mountain:

1. $\neg \exists x$ (x is golden $\wedge$ x is a mountain $\wedge$ x exists).
2. The Existent Golden Mountain is determined as being a mountain, as being golden, and as being existent/existing.[84] (According to CP.)
3. The Existent Golden Mountain is determined as being existent/existing. (2)

3 does not entail that The Existent Golden Mountain *is* existent/exists. Therefore, it cannot be derived that there is something that is golden and a mountain and exists. No contradiction arises.

The problem of nonperceivability does not arise for modes-of-predication theories. Since Meinongian objects are considered to be abstract objects, it goes without saying that they are not perceivable. Nonperceivability belongs to the

---

[83] A special case is Castañeda's settist abstract Meinongianism. According to it, "Meinongian predication" (Castañeda's term!) is set membership (Castañeda (1972): 51f.). However, this is also supposed to be a relation between properties and individuals, since, according to Castañeda, individuals just *are* sets of properties.

[84] With the modes-of-predication distinction at hand, there is no more need for Meinong's terminological distinction between "exists" and "is existent". The job of "is existent" is done by "is determined as being existing".

very nature of abstract objects. Consequently, it is simply not possible that a Meinongian object *is* a mountain. It is, however, possible that a Meinongian object *is determined as* a mountain. However, being determined as being a mountain does not entail perceivability; neither does being determined as being blue, or any other determined-as predicate.

The modes-of-predication distinction also sheds new light on the problem of excluded middle and the problem of noncontradiction. In a Meinongian spirit, it should be postulated (1) that nonexistent objects are only incomplete with respect to is-determined-as predicates, and (2) that nonexistent objects are only contradictory with respect to is-determined-as predicates. Thus, it holds:

(Inc) $\forall x$ (x is an incompletely determined object $\leftrightarrow \exists \varphi$ ($\neg$ (x is determined as φ $\lor$ x is determined as $\overline{\varphi}$))).[85]

(Read: For all x: x is an incompletely determined object if, and only if: there is a φ, such that: it is not the case that x is determined as φ or x is determined as non-φ. For instance, The Blue is neither determined as rectangular nor as non-rectangular.)

(Contr) $\forall x$ (x is a contradictory object $\leftrightarrow \exists \varphi$ (x is determined as $\varphi \land x$ is determined as $\overline{\varphi}$)).

(Read: For all x: x is a contradictory object if, and only if, there is a φ, such that x is determined as φ, and x is determined as non-φ. For instance, The Round Square is both determined as round and as non-round.)

However, this does not entail that, for an incomplete object x, there is some φ, such that neither "x is φ" nor "x is $\overline{\varphi}$" is true. It also does not entail that for a contradictory object x, that there is some φ, such that both "x is φ" and "x is $\overline{\varphi}$" are true. It is true, for instance, that The Blue *is* non-rectangular; and it is false that The Round Square *is* both round and square.

A modes-of-predication distinction can be represented, without the introduction of new symbols, by syntactical means. Using an elegant symbolism introduced by Edward N. Zalta (1983, 1988), one can represent "*a* is determined as F" as "*a*F", in contrast to "F*a*", which expresses the familiar predication "*a* is F" (similarly Castañeda, 1972: 52). In the spirit of neo-Meinongians like Castañeda and Zalta, one can formulate, among others, the following principles:

$\forall \varphi \exists x \, (\varphi x)$

(Read: For every φ, there is an x, such that x is determined as φ.)

---

[85] For the use of "φ", see note 35 in Subsection 2.2.

$\forall \varphi \, \exists x \, (\neg \varphi x \wedge \neg \overline{\varphi} x)$

(Read: For every φ, there is an x, such that x is not determined as φ, and x is not determined as non-φ.)

$\forall \varphi \, \exists x \, (\varphi x \wedge \overline{\varphi} x)$

(Read: For every φ, there is an x, such that x is determined as φ, and x is determined as non-φ.)

5.4.3 Modal Meinongianism and the Other Worlds Strategy

The term "Modal Meinongianism" was coined by Francesco Berto, who is, along with Graham Priest, one of the main proponents of this view. Priest calls the view "noneism" – a term he takes from Richard Routley. According to Modal Meinongianism, "concrete objects exist; everything else (abstract objects, worlds, merely possible objects, impossible objects) simply do not exist" (Priest, 2005: vii), but they nevertheless have intrinsic properties and stand in relations to other objects (nonexistent as well as existent ones). Modal Meinongians do not distinguish between any modes of being. They do not make a semantic distinction between "there is" and "exists". Accordingly, they do not accept the principle that there are nonexistent objects. Therefore, Modal Meinongianism is not a variety of Meinongianism, in the sense of the concept of Meinongianism as defined in Section 1. (For another deviation from Meinongianism, see note 86.)

Modal Meinongianism rests on the assumption that there are (in an ontologically neutral sense of "there are"!) worlds over and above the actual world (possible as well as impossible ones). All worlds are supposed to share the same domain. But not all objects of the domain are supposed to exist in all possible worlds. According to Modal Meinongianism, The Golden Mountain exists in some possible but nonactual worlds.

According to the other worlds strategy, nonexistent objects literally *have* the properties by which they are "characterized" – but they have these properties not in the actual world, but only in those worlds "which realize the way the objects are represented as being in the appropriate cognitive state ..." (Priest, 2011b: 249, note 35). Suppose you imagine a winged horse. In this case, in your imagination, you have an intentional object that is represented as being winged and a horse. Thus, the intentional object of your present intentional state is a nonexistent winged horse, which is, however, in the actual world neither winged nor a horse. At some worlds, however, this object is winged and a horse – namely, in those worlds which realize the way the object is represented in your imagination.

Why can't we simply say that nonexistent objects have the properties they are characterized as having in the worlds in which they exist? Priest explains that this is not his view, since, according to his brand of Modal Meinongianism, "[t]hey may not exist at such worlds – indeed it may be part of their characterization that they do not exist. Conversely, they may exist at worlds without having their characterizing properties there: there are worlds where Sherlock Holmes exists and is a doctor, not a detective" (Priest, 2011b: 249, note 35). That is, a nonexistent object that is an existent detective at one nonactual world may be identical to a nonexistent object that is an existent doctor at another nonactual world.

Priest distinguishes properties that are "existence-entailing" from properties that are not existence-entailing. Exactly which properties are existence-entailing and which are not is a tricky question (reminiscent of the question of which properties are nuclear and which are extranuclear). But some examples may provide an idea. Existence-entailing properties are, for instance: being a planet, standing in a doorway, being kicked by someone, being golden, being a mountain.[86]

Thus, Sherlock Holmes is indeed a detective and lives in Baker Street – but not in the actual world, but in those nonactual possible worlds "that realize the way [a reader] represent[s] the world to be when [she] read[s] the Holmes stories" (Priest, 2005: 84). Similarly, The Golden Mountain is golden and a mountain in those nonactual possible worlds that realize the way someone represents the world to be when she is imagining The Golden Mountain; and The Round Square is round and square in those *impossible* nonactual worlds that realize the way someone represents the world to be when she is thinking about The Round Square.

Consequently, Modal Meinongian logic involves quantification over worlds, both possible and impossible ones, so that one can express not only that some formula is true (or false) *simpliciter* but that it is true or false in some world w. Accordingly, the formal language of Modal Meinongian logic contains variables and constants for worlds and a syntax for expressions like "a is F at some world w" (Priest, 2005: section 1.3).

Modal Meinongianism can resolve both the paradox of The Existent Golden Mountain and the problem of nonperceivability in a straightforward way: Given that being golden and being a mountain are existence-entailing

---

[86] The distinction between properties which entail existence and properties that do not can also be found in Cocchiarella (1969), who mentions Richard Montague as the originator of this distinction (see notes 2 and 3 on p. 33 and note 4 on p. 35). Incidentally, the postulation of existence-entailing properties is an implicit rejection of Meinong's principle of independence (IP). In Section 1, I postulated IP as one of the essential features of Meinongianism. Hence, in this regard too, Modal Meinongianism is not a kind of Meinongianism, as defined in Section 1.

properties, The Existent Golden Mountain is indeed existent (and exists) at those possible worlds which realize the way we imagine it (namely, as being existent, being golden, and being a mountain). In those worlds which do not realize the way we imagine The Golden Mountain, it does not exist. But in these worlds, it is neither golden nor a mountain nor existent. Thus, the contradiction is avoided. Concerning perceivability, The Golden Mountain is indeed perceivable at all those worlds in which it is both golden and a mountain.

Modal Meinongianism has given rise to extensive discussion.[87] Among other things, one may be worried about the underlying conception of trans-world identity: What makes an object that is a nonexistent x in the actual world identical with an existent y in some nonactual worlds, given that x and y have hardly any properties in common? Related to this is an objection voiced in Bueno and Zalta (2017): "It is not just that, at different worlds, different objects might realize the way Holmes is represented, but also that the modal Meinongian's characterization principle doesn't guarantee, at *any* world, that there is a unique object that satisfies there the characterization of the Conan Doyle novels" (762f.). Moreover, it is not easy to understand that objects *exist* in some nonactual worlds, although these nonactual worlds themselves do not exist (and do not have any other kind of being). One might also object to the Modal Meinongian conception of fictitious objects that it seems that we use the name "Sherlock Holmes" to refer to a fictitious character in the actual world, not to a real person in some nonactual worlds.

5.4.4 A Plea for Modes of Predication

With the exception of Modal Meinongians (who shall be put aside for the moment), all neo-Meinongians make use either of the distinction between nuclear and extranuclear properties or of a modes-of-predication distinction in order to resolve certain problems of Meinongianism. But which solution is better?

It was shown that the nuclear–extranuclear distinction in its most simple version cannot resolve the problem of nonperceivability. It also cannot provide a satisfying solution to the paradox of The Existent Golden Mountain. The latter can be repaired with the additional assumption that, for every extranuclear property, there is a nuclear counterpart. The former could also be repaired by means of an additional amendment, namely the assumption *that for every nuclear property, there is an extranuclear counterpart*. Given this additional assumption, we could say that nuclear properties are *never* perceivability-entailing – only their

---

[87] For critical comments, see Hale (2007); Kroon (2008 and 2012); Nolan (2008); Reicher (2008); Bueno and Zalta (2017). Priest replies to some of these criticisms in Priest (2008 and 2011b). For further defenses of Priest, see Barz (2016) and de Jong (2021).

extranuclear counterparts are. Accordingly, we could say that an object that has the nuclear property of being a mountain is not perceivable, in contrast to an object that has the extranuclear property of being a mountain. Thus, Mount Everest has the extranuclear property of being a mountain, whereas The Golden Mountain (as well as The Existent Golden Mountain, of course) has the nuclear property of being a mountain. In general, we could say: Nuclear properties are exemplified by *types* only. Types exemplify both nuclear and extranuclear properties. Concrete objects exemplify only extranuclear properties.

To my knowledge, *this* version of the nuclear–extranuclear distinction has not yet been supported by any existing or past Meinongian, except Meinong himself. But it would work fine – at least better than the simple version and Parsons's partly refined version. However, if the nuclear–extranuclear distinction is construed in this way, it becomes equivalent to the modes-of-predication distinction in the following sense: Each sentence that makes use of the nuclear–extranuclear distinction can be rendered such that it makes use of the modes-of-predication distinction instead, and vice versa.[88] Consider:

The Golden Mountain has the nuclear property of being a mountain.
The Golden Mountain is determined as being a mountain.

The Golden Mountain does not have the extranuclear property of being a mountain.
The Golden Mountain is not a mountain.

Mount Everest has the extranuclear property of being a mountain.
Mount Everest is a mountain.

The Existent Golden Mountain has the nuclear property of being existent.
The Existent Golden Mountain is determined as being existent.

The Existent Golden Mountain does not have the extranuclear property of being existent.
The Existent Golden Mountain is not existent/does not exist.

Sherlock Holmes has the nuclear property of being a detective.
Sherlock Holmes is determined as being a detective.

Sherlock Holmes does not have the extranuclear property of being a detective.
Sherlock Holmes is not a detective.

Sherlock Holmes has the extranuclear property of being a fictitious character.
Sherlock Holmes is a fictitious character.

---

[88] For an interpretation of the nuclear–extranuclear distinction as functionally equivalent to the modes-of-predication distinction, see Fine (1984: 98); Reicher (2006: section IV).

Let us call the first of each of these pairs of sentences an "N-E sentence" (for "nuclear–extranuclear") and the second a "MP sentence" (for "modes of predication"). A Meinongian theory that entails these N–E sentences has exactly the same explanatory force as a Meinongian theory that entails the MP sentences. In this sense, the two distinctions are functionally equivalent.

However, this does not imply that the N–E sentences *have the same meaning* as the MP sentences. There is a difference in the ontological implications: N–E sentences entail an ontological commitment to properties; MP sentences do not entail such a commitment. Given the principle that, from two theories that have the same explanatory force, one should choose the ontologically more parsimonious one, it is clear that the choice should fall on the modes-of-predication distinction.

Recently, the modes-of-predication distinction has come under attack from Modal Meinongians. (See Berto, 2013; Priest, 2016; for replies, see Bueno and Zalta, 2017.) The following objections, among others, have been raised:

(1) The modes-of-predication distinction is ad hoc.
(2) The modes-of-predication distinction is vague and obscure.
(3) It is counterintuitive to consider fictitious characters as abstract objects.

I will now provide some short replies to these objections.

Reply to (1). The modes-of-predication distinction has a long history in philosophy. Apart from the Meinongians who make use of this distinction (see the beginning of Subsection 5.4.2), it can also be found in a variety of non-Meinongian theories: in ontological theories of art works (e.g., Ingarden, 1931/2012; Wolterstorff, 1980), in theories of fictitious objects as abstract artifacts (e.g., van Inwagen, 1977; Voltolini, 2006), and arguably even in Plato (see Bueno and Zalta, 2017: section 4). These theories are consistent and comprehensive and have manifold applications. The modes-of-predication distinction is essential for their consistency and fruitfulness. Therefore, the modes-of-predication distinction is not ad hoc.

Reply to (2). Admittedly, the modes-of-predication distinction may initially seem mysterious. However, the mists evaporate when Meinongian objects are understood as *types*, that is, as universals (distinct from properties) that can be realized in concrete particulars (unless they are determined in a contradictory way). (Cf. Subsection 4.3, on Meinong's theory of implexive being.) The Meinongian incomplete object The Mountain is realized in every mountain; the Meinongian incomplete object The Golden Mountain is not realized in any mountain, but it could be realized, if there were an object that is both golden and a mountain.

The copula "is determined as" cannot be defined any more than the familiar copula "is". However, it can be elucidated by an explication of the relation between the concept of being determined as such-and-such and the concept of being a realization of a type:

(D) For all types t and for all φ: If t *is determined as* φ, then, for all x: if x is a realization of t, then x *is* φ.

(D) $\forall t \Pi \varphi$ (t is determined as $\varphi \rightarrow \forall x$ ($Rxt \rightarrow x$ is φ)).

If some t is determined as a mountain and golden, every realization of t is both a mountain and golden. The following, however, does not hold:

(D*) $\forall t \Pi \varphi$ (t is determined as $\varphi \leftrightarrow \forall x$ ($Rxt \rightarrow x$ is φ)).

D* does not hold for the following reason: If t does not have any realization (as with The Golden Mountain), "$Rxt \rightarrow x$ is φ" is trivially true for all x and all φ, but this does not entail that "t is determined as φ" is true for any φ.

It should be noted that this explanation does not only shed light on one of the basic concepts of Meinongianism, but also on one of the perennial problems of Platonism, raised for the first time by Plato himself in the dialogue *Parmenides*: How can we understand the relation between an idea (say, the idea of man) and the individuals who "partake" in the idea (i.e., its instances, the individual men)? The answer is: The idea is not similar to its instances, in the sense that idea and instances have common properties (and, of course, the idea is not divided between the individuals, like a cake may be divided between party guests). The idea rather determines those properties of its instances that are essential for being instances of it, such that, for all φ, if the idea of man is determined as φ, then every man is φ.

The modes-of-predication distinction also provides a straightforward identity condition for types: A type t_1 is identical to a type t_2, if, and only if: for all φ: t_1 is determined as φ iff t_2 is determined as φ. Thus, the modes-of-predication distinction allows for answering tricky questions about the identity of fictitious characters, such as: Is Goethe's Faust character identical to Marlowe's Faust character? (The short answer is: No, because there are some φ, such that Goethe's Faust is determined as φ, but Marlowe's Faust is not – and vice versa.)[89] Incidentally, it also allows for answering Quine's questions about the

---

[89] However, Goethe's and Marlowe's Faust character may have a "logical part" in common. I use the term "logical part" here in the following sense: Type t_1 is a (proper) logical part of type t_2 if, and only if, for some (but not for all) φ: If t_2 is determined as φ, then t_1 is determined as φ. For

possible men in the doorway (Quine, 1948/1953): The Possible Fat Man in the Doorway is, of course, not identical to The Bald Man in the Doorway, since the Possible Fat Man in the Doorway is determined as being fat and not as being bold, and vice versa.

I cannot see any "vagueness" in the modes-of-predication distinction. Moreover, the modes-of-predication distinction can easily be made intuitively plausible, in particular concerning fictitious objects, in the following way (in Zalta's terminology): A fictitious character encodes exactly those properties that it has *according to the relevant story*.[90] To put it in terms of determination: A fictitious character is determined as φ if, and only if, the character is φ according to the story. So the modes-of-predication distinction is no more obscure than the conception of being such-and-such according to a story – a conception that most people (not only trained philosophers) can easily comprehend.

Reply to (3): Obviously, intuitions about the nature of fictitious objects vary, in particular among philosophers. However, many philosophers (including myself) and also many laypeople find the conception of fictitious characters as abstract objects highly intuitive, especially in light of a broader theory of literary works. I dare say that nowadays the view that fictitious characters are abstract objects is the view of the majority of philosophers who work on the ontology of fiction.[91]

5.5 Summary and Closing Remarks

In its origins, Meinongian object theory was primarily intended as a solution for the problem of intentionality: If every intentional attitude has an object, but some intentional attitudes do not have an existent object, there must be nonexistent objects. A second important motivation for object theory was the problem of negative singular existence statements: If "The winged horse does not exist" is a true statement, the subject term "the winged horse" cannot refer to an existent object. Therefore, it must refer to a nonexistent object.

Soon after its appearance, Bertrand Russell blamed object theory for violating basic logical principles, such as the principle of excluded middle and the principle of noncontradiction. In reaction to this, Meinong made important

---

instance, The Mountain is a proper logical part of The Golden Mountain. (Cf. note 64 in Subsection 4.3.) To put it loosely: Goethe's Faust and Marlowe's Faust share some, but not all, of their determinations; they are distinct but overlapping.

[90] For a detailed analysis of "according to a story", see Reicher (2006).

[91] Not all of them are Meinongians, of course. The view that fictitious characters belong to the category of abstract artifacts is far more popular. See note 19 in Subsection 1.2.3 for references.

amendments. In doing so, he at least paved the way for a consistent version of object theory. Nevertheless, Russell's harsh verdict remained unchallenged for some decades, at least in analytic philosophy.

It was only in the 1970s that the tide turned in favor of Meinongianism. Starting with Roderick M. Chisholm, analytic philosophers rediscovered object theory and recognized its explanatory power, not only for the problems of intentionality and negative singular existence statements, but also for a larger variety of applications, including the problem of fictitious objects and the problem of past and future objects. It was shown, often by means of formal logic, that Meinongianism can be modeled as a consistent theory. No doubt Russell's objections are refuted.

However, the question remains whether Meinongianism is really the best solution to all or some of the problems outlined in this Element (intentionality, negative singular existence statements, fictitious objects, past and future, and others). As always in philosophy, there are alternative solutions around. The debate continues.

References

Abell, C. (2020). *Fiction: A Philosophical Analysis*, Oxford: Oxford University Press.

Austin, J. L. (1979). *Philosophical Papers*. Ed. by J. O. Urmson and G. J. Warnock. 3rd ed., Oxford: Clarendon.

Azzouni, J. (2013). Hobnobbing with the nonexistent. *Inquiry*, 56(4), 340–358.

Bach, K. (1985–86). Failed reference and feigned reference: Much ado about nothing. *Grazer Philosophische Studien*, 25/26, 359–374.

Barnes, J. (1972). *The Ontological Argument*, London: Macmillan.

Barz, W. (2016). Two-dimensional Modal Meinongianism. *Ratio* (new series), 29, 249–267.

Berto, F. (2008). Modal Meinongianism for fictional objects. *Metaphysica*, 9, 205–218.

Berto, F. (2011). Modal Meinongianism and fiction: The best of three worlds. *Philosophical Studies*, 152(3), 313–334.

Berto, F. (2013). *Existence as a Real Property: The Ontology of Meinongianism*, Dordrecht: Springer.

Bertolet, R. (1984). Reference, fiction, and fictions. *Synthese*, 60, 413–437.

Braithwaite, R. B. (1933). Symposium: Imaginary objects. *Proceedings of the Aristotelian Society*, Supp. vol. 12, 44–54.

Brentano, F. (1874). *Psychologie vom empirischen Standpunkt*, Leipzig: Duncker & Humblot. [Translation: *Psychology from an Empirical Standpoint.*]

Brock, S. (2002). Fictionalism about fictional characters. *Noûs*, 36(1), 1–21.

Bueno, O. and Zalta, E. N. (2017). Object theory and Modal Meinongianism. *Australasian Journal of Philosophy*, 95(4), 761–778. https://doi.org/10.1080/00048402.2016.1260609.

Carnap, R. (1950). Empiricism, semantics, and ontology. *Revue Internationale de Philosophie*, 4, 20–40.

Castañeda, H.-N. (1972). Thinking and the structure of the world, *Critica*, 6, 43–86.

Castañeda, H.-N. (1979). Fiction and reality: Their fundamental connections. *Poetics*, 8, 31–62.

Centrone, S. (2016). Relational theories of intentionality and the problem of non-existents. In M. Antonelli and M. David, eds., *Existence, Fiction, Assumption: Meinongian Themes and the History of Austrian Philosophy*. Berlin: de Gruyter, 1–26.

Chisholm, R. M. (1972). Beyond being and nonbeing. In R. Haller, ed., *Jenseits von Sein und Nichtsein: Beiträge zur Meinong-Forschung*. Graz: Akademische Druck- und Verlagsanstalt, 25–33. [Published also, only slightly revised, in *Philosophical Studies*, 24(4), 1973, 245–257, and in R. M. Chisholm, *Brentano and Meinong Studies*. Amsterdam: Rodopi, 1982, 53–67.]

Cocchiarella, N. B. (1969). Existence entailing attributes, modes of copulation and modes of being in second order logic. *Noûs*, 3, 33–48.

Crane, T. (2001). Intentional objects. *Ratio*, 14, 336–349.

Crane, T. (2012). What is the problem of non-existence? *Philosophia: Philosophical Quarterly of Israel*, 40(3), 417–434.

Crane, T. (2013). *The Objects of Thought*, Oxford: Oxford University Press.

Crittenden, C. (1973). Thinking about non-being. *Inquiry*, 16, 290–312.

Cumming, S. (2019). Names. In E. N. Zalta, ed., *The Stanford Encyclopedia of Philosophy* (Fall 2019 Edition), https://plato.stanford.edu/archives/fall2019/entries/names/.

Currie, G. (1990). *The Nature of Fiction*, New York: Cambridge University Press.

de Jong, A. (2021). Now, imagine an actually existing unicorn: On Russellian worries for Modal Meinongianism. *Axiomathes*, 31(3), 365–380.

Dölling, E. (2001). Alexius Meinong's life and work. In L. Albertazzi, D. Jacquette, and R. Poli, eds., *The School of Alexius Meinong*. Aldershot: Ashgate, 49–76.

Eklund, M. (2006). Metaontology. *Philosophy Compass*, 1(3), 317–334.

Eklund, M. (2019). Fictionalism. In E. N. Zalta, ed., *The Stanford Encyclopedia of Philosophy* (Winter 2019 edition), https://plato.stanford.edu/archives/win2019/entries/fictionalism/.

Everett, A. (2005). Against fictional realism. *Journal of Philosophy*, 102, 624–649.

Everett, A. (2013). *The Nonexistent*, Oxford: Oxford University Press.

Findlay, J. N. (1963). *Meinong's Theory of Objects and Values*, London: Oxford University Press. [Revised and extended version of *Meinong's Theory of Objects* from 1933.]

Fine, K. (1982). The problem of non-existents. I. Internalism. *Topoi*, 1, 97–140.

Fine, K. (1983). Symposium: A defence of arbitrary objects, I. *Proceedings of the Aristotelian Society*, Suppl. Vol. 57, 55–77.

Fine, K. (1984). Critical review of Parsons' *Nonexistent Objects*. *Philosophical Studies*, 45, 94–142.

Frege, G. (1891/2021). Function und Begriff. In G. Frege, *Ausgewählte Schriften zur Philosophie der Logik und der Sprache*, ed. by D. Rami. Göttingen: Vandenhoeck & Ruprecht, 89–106. [Originally published 1891 in Jena by Pohle. English translation: Function and concept. In P. Geach and M. Black, eds. and transl., *Translations from the Philosophical Writings of Gottlob Frege*. Oxford: Blackwell, 3rd ed. 1980, 21–41. The German original is open access available at https://books.google.de/books?id=BtwEAAAAYAAJ&redir_esc=y&hl=de.]

Frege, G. (1892a/2021). Ueber Begriff und Gegenstand. In G. Frege, *Ausgewählte Schriften zur Philosophie der Logik und der Sprache*, ed. by D. Rami. Göttingen: Vandenhoeck & Ruprecht, 126–137. [Originally published in 1892 in *Vierteljahresschrift für wissenschaftliche Philosophie*, 16, 197–205. English translation: Concept and object. In P. Geach and M. Black, eds. and transl., *Translations from the Philosophical Writings of Gottlob Frege*. Oxford: Blackwell, 3rd ed. 1980, 42–55.]

Frege, G. (1892b/2021). Über Sinn und Bedeutung. In G. Frege, *Ausgewählte Schriften zur Philosophie der Logik und der Sprache*, ed. by D. Rami. Göttingen: Vandenhoeck & Ruprecht, 107–125. [Originally published in *Zeitschrift für Philosophie und philosophische Kritik*, N. F., 100/I, 1892, 25–50. English translation: On sense and reference. In P. Geach and M. Black, eds. and transl., *Translations from the Philosophical Writings of Gottlob Frege*. Oxford: Blackwell, 3rd ed. 1980, 56–78.]

Frege, G. (2021a). Dialog mit Pünjer über Existenz. In G. Frege, *Ausgewählte Schriften zur Philosophie der Logik und der Sprache*, ed. by D. Rami. Göttingen: Vandenhoeck & Ruprecht, 71–77. [Published only posthumously.]

Frege, G. (2021b). Auseinandersetzung mit Pünjer über Existenz. In G. Frege, *Ausgewählte Schriften zur Philosophie der Logik und der Sprache*, ed. by D. Rami. Göttingen: Vandenhoeck & Ruprecht, 78–84. [Published only posthumously.]

Gan, N. (2021). Fictionalism and Meinongianism. *Theoria: Revista de Teoria, Historia y Fundamentos de la Ciencia*, 36(1), 49–62.

Geach, P. T. (1951). Symposion: On what there is. I. *Proceedings of the Aristotelian Society*, Suppl. Vol. 25, 125–136.

Gorman, M. (2006). Talking about intentional objects. *Dialectica*, 60(2), 135–144.

Griffin, N. (1977). Russell's "horrible travesty" of Meinong. *Russell: The Journal of the Bertrand Russell Studies*, 97, 39–51.

Griffin, N. (1985–86). Russell's critique of Meinong's theory of objects. In R. Haller, ed., *Non-Existence and Predication*. Amsterdam: Rodopi (= *Grazer Philosophische Studien*, 25/26), 375–401.

Grossmann, R. (2001). Meinong's main mistake. In L. Albertazzi, D. Jacquette, and R. Poli, eds., *The School of Alexius Meinong*. Aldershot: Ashgate, 477–488.

Hale, B. (2007). "Into the abyss": A critical study of Graham Priest: *Towards Non-being: The Logics and Metaphysics of Intentionality*. *Philosophia Mathematica*, 15, 94–110.

Hicks, G. D. (1922). The philosophical researches of Meinong (I.). *Mind* (n.s.), 31(121), 1–30.

Hinchliff, M. (1988). *A Defense of Presentism*. Doctoral dissertation, Princeton University.

Hofweber, T. (2000). Quantification and non-existent objects. In A. Everett and T. Hofweber, eds., *Empty Names, Fiction, and the Puzzles of Non-existence*. Stanford, CA: CSLI Publications, 249–273.

Ingarden, R. (1931/2012). *Das literarische Kunstwerk*, Tübingen: Niemeyer. Most recent edition: de Gruyter, 2012 (reprint of the 4th edition from 1972). [English translation: *The Literary Work of Art*, Evanston, IL: Northwestern University Press, 1973.]

Jackson, F. (1980). Ontological commitment and paraphrase. *Philosophy: The Journal of the Royal Institute of Philosophy*, 55, 303–315.

Jacquette, D. (1989). Intentional semantics and the logic of fiction. *British Journal of Aesthetics*, 29, 168–176.

Jacquette, D. (1996). *Meinongian Logic: The Semantics of Existence and Nonexistence*, Berlin: de Gruyter.

Jorgensen, A. K. (2002). Meinong's much maligned modal moment. *Grazer Philosophische Studien*, 64, 95–118.

Kant, I. (1763/2011). *Der einzig mögliche Beweisgrund zu einer Demonstration des Daseins Gottes*. Hamburg: Meiner. [First edition 1763.] The text of the *Akademie-Ausgabe* is open access available at https://korpora.zim.uni-duis burg-essen.de/kant/aa02/063.html.

Kant, I. (1787/1929). *Critique of Pure Reason*. Transl. by N. K. Smith. London: Macmillan. This edition is open access available at https://ia800706.us .archive.org/13/items/immanuelkantscri032379mbp/immanuelkantscri032379 mbp.pdf.

Kapitan, T. (1990). Preserving a robust sense of reality. In K. Jacobi and H. Pape, eds., *Thinking and the Structure of the World: Hector-Neri Castañeda's Epistemic Ontology Presented and Criticized*. Berlin: de Gruyter, 449–458.

Kripke, S. A. (1980). *Naming and Necessity*, Cambridge, MA: Harvard University Press.

Kroon, F. W. (1996). Characterizing non-existents. *Grazer Philosophische Studien*, 51, 163–193.

Kroon, F. (2008). Much ado about nothing: Priest and the reinvention of noneism. *Philosophy and Phenomenological Research*, 76, 199–207.

Kroon, F. (2011). The fiction of creationism. In F. Lihoreau, ed., *Truth in Fiction*. Heusenstamm: Ontos, 203–221.

Kroon, F. (2012). Characterization and existence in Modal Meinongianism. *Grazer Philosophische Studien*, 86, 23–34.

Künne, W. (1990). Perception, fiction, and elliptical speech. In K. Jacobi and H. Pape, eds., *Thinking and the Structure of the World: Hector-Neri*

Castañeda's Epistemic Ontology Presented and Criticized. Berlin: de Gruyter, 259–267.

Lambert, K. (1983). *Meinong and the Principle of Independence: Its Place in Meinong's Theory of Objects and its Significance in Contemporary Philosophical Logic*, Cambridge: Cambridge University Press.

Lambert, K. (1991). The nature of Free Logic. In Lambert, *Philosophical Applications of Free Logic*, Oxford: Oxford University Press, 3–14.

Landini, G. (2017). Meinong and Russell: Some lessons on quantification. *Axiomathes*, 27(5), 455–474.

Leblanc, H., and Hailperin, T. (1959). Nondesignating singular terms. *Philosophical Review*, 68, 239–243.

Lejewski, C. (1954). Logic and existence. *British Journal for the Philosophy of Science*, 5, 104–119.

Leonard, H. S. (1956). The logic of existence. *Philosophical Studies*, 7, 49–64.

Lewis, D. (1990). Noneism or allism? *Mind*, 99, 23–31.

Linsky, B. (2014). Ernst Mally's anticipation of encoding. *Journal for the History of Analytic Philosophy*, 2(5). https://doi.org/10.15173/jhap.v2i5.40.

Linsky, L. (1972). Two concepts of quantification. *Noûs*, 6, 224–239.

Macdonald, M. (1954). The language of fiction. *Proceedings of the Aristotelian Society*, Supp. Vol. 27, 165–184. [Reprint in F. Tillman and S. M. Cahn, eds., *Philosophy of Art and Aesthetics: From Plato to Wittgenstein*, New York: Harper and Row, 1969, 617–630.]

Mally, E. (1912). *Gegenstandstheoretische Grundlagen der Logik und Logistik*, Leipzig: Barth.

Marcus, R. B. (1962). Interpreting quantification. *Inquiry*, 5, 252–259.

Marek, J. (2022). Alexius Meinong. In E. N. Zalta, ed., *The Stanford Encyclopedia of Philosophy* (Fall 2019 Edition), https://plato.stanford.edu/archives/fall2022/entries/meinong/.

Meinong, A. (1904/1960). Über Gegenstandstheorie. In A. Meinong, ed., *Untersuchungen zur Gegenstandstheorie und Psychologie*. Leipzig: Barth, 1–50. The original edition of the whole volume is open access available at https://archive.org/details/untersuchungenzu00mein/page/50/mode/2up, and it has been reprinted under the original title (Norderstedt: Verlag der Wissenschaften, 2015). The paper "Über Gegenstandstheorie" has been reprinted in *Alexius Meinong Gesamtausgabe*, ed. by R. Haller and R. Kindinger, together with R. Chisholm, vol. II: *Abhandlungen zur Erkenntnistheorie und Gegenstandstheorie*. Graz: Akademische Druck- und Verlagsanstalt, 1971, pp. 481–535. Transl. as "The theory of objects" in R. M. Chisholm (ed.), *Realism and the Background of Phenomenology*. Glencoe, IL: Free Press, 1960; reprint: Atascadero, CA: Ridgeview, 1981, 76–117.

Meinong, A. (1907/1973). *Über die Stellung der Gegenstandstheorie im System der Wissenschaften.* Leipzig: Voigtländer. The original edition of this work is open access available at https://archive.org/details/berdiestellungd00mein goog. It has been reprinted in *Alexius Meinong Gesamtausgabe,* ed. by R. Haller and R. Kindinger, together with R. Chisholm, vol. V. Graz: Akademische Druck- und Verlagsanstalt, 1973.

Meinong, A. (1908/1978). Über Inhalt und Gegenstand. In R. Fabian and R. Haller, eds., *Kolleghefte und Fragmente. Schriften aus dem Nachlaß* (=*Ergänzungsband* to *Alexius Meinong Gesamtausgabe*). Graz: Akademische Druck- und Verlagsanstalt 1978, 145–159. [Written in 1908; only posthumously published.]

Meinong, A. (1910/1968). *Über Annahmen* (second, revised edition). Leipzig: Barth, 1910. Vol. IV of *Alexius Meinong Gesamtausgabe,* ed. by R. Haller and R. Kindinger, together with R. Chisholm. Graz: Akademische Druck- und Verlagsanstalt, 1968. English translation: *On Assumptions.* Transl. with an introduction by J. Heanue. Berkeley, CA: University of California Press, 1983. The original from 1910 is open access available at https://archive.org/details/b28066820.

Meinong, A. (1913/1978). Zweites Kolleg über gegenstandstheoretische Logik. In R. Fabian and R. Haller, eds., *Kolleghefte und Fragmente: Schriften aus dem Nachlaß* (=*Ergänzungsband* to *Alexius Meinong Gesamtausgabe*). Graz: Akademische Druck- und Verlagsanstalt 1978, 237–272. [Written in 1913; only posthumously published.]

Meinong, A. (1915/1972). *Über Möglichkeit und Wahrscheinlichkeit.* Leipzig: Barth. Reprinted as vol. VI of *Alexius Meinong Gesamtausgabe,* ed. by R. Haller and R. Kindinger, together with R. Chisholm. Graz: Akademische Druck- und Verlagsanstalt, 1972.

Meinong, A. (1917/1968). *Über emotionale Präsentation.* Sitzungsberichte der philosophisch-historischen Klasse der Kaiserlichen Akademie der Wissenschaften in Wien, 183. Band, 2. Abhandlung. Reprinted in R. Haller and R. Kindinger, eds., *Alexius Meinong Gesamtausgabe,* vol. III. Graz: Akademische Druck- und Verlagsanstalt, 1968, 285–465. [English translation: *On Emotional Presentation,* Evanston, IL: Northwestern University Press.]

Meinong, A. (1917–18/1978). Viertes Kolleg über Erkenntnistheorie. In R. Fabian and R. Haller, eds., *Kolleghefte und Fragmente. Schriften aus dem Nachlaß* (=*Ergänzungsband* to *Alexius Meinong Gesamtausgabe*). Graz: Akademische Druck- und Verlagsanstalt 1978, 337–401. [Written in 1917–1918; only posthumously published.]

Meinong, A. 1921/1978: Selbstdarstellung. In R. Schmidt, ed., *Die deutsche Philosophie der Gegenwart in Selbstdarstellungen,* vol. 1. Leipzig: Meiner,

1921, 91–150. Reprinted in R. Haller and R. Kindinger, together with R. M. Chisholm, eds., vol. VII of *Alexius Meinong Gesamtausgabe* (*Selbstdarstellung. Vermischte Schriften*). Graz: Akademische Druck- und Verlagsanstalt, 1978. Partial translation in R. Grossmann, *Meinong*. London: Routledge & Kegan Paul, 1974, 224–236.

Miravalle, J.-M. L. (2019). *God, Existence, and Fictional Objects: The Case for Meinongian Theism*, London: Bloomsbury.

Nolan, D. (2008). Properties and paradox in Graham Priest's *Towards Non-Being*. *Philosophy and Phenomenological Research*, 76, 191–198.

Paoletti, M. P. (2015). A problem for ontological pluralism and a half-Meinongian solution. *Philosophia: Philosophical Quarterly of Israel*, 43(2), 463–473.

Parsons, T. (1975). A Meinongian analysis of fictional objects. *Grazer Philosophische Studien*, 1, 73–86.

Parsons, T. (1980). *Nonexistent Objects*, New Haven, CT: Yale University Press.

Parsons, T. (1995). Meinongian semantics generalized. *Grazer Philosophische Studien*, 50, 145–161.

Paśniczek, J. (1998). *The Logic of Intentional Objects: A Meinongian Version of Classical Logic*, Dordrecht: Kluwer.

Perszyk, K. J. (1993). *Nonexistent Objects: Meinong and Contemporary Philosophy*, Dordrecht: Kluwer.

Peters, S. (2008). Symmetry and other relational properties of type <1, 1> quantifiers. In S. Peters and D. Westerståhl, eds., *Quantifiers in Language and Logic*. Oxford: Oxford University Press, 208–241. https://doi.org/ 10.1093/acprof:oso/9780199291267.001.0001.

Priest, G. (2005). *Towards Non-Being: The Logic and Metaphysics of Intentionality*, Oxford: Clarendon Press. [Second, revised and extended edition: 2016.]

Priest, G. (2008). Replies to Nolan and Kroon. *Philosophy and Phenomenological Research*, 76, 208–214.

Priest, G. (2011a). Creating non-existents. In F. Lihoreau, ed., *Truth in Fiction*. Heusenstamm: Ontos, 107–118.

Priest, G. (2011b). Against against nonbeing. *Review of Symbolic Logic*, 4(2), 237–253.

Priest, G. (2016). *Towards Non-Being: The Logic and Metaphysics of Intentionality*, 2nd ed., Oxford: Oxford University Press. [Extended and revised edition of Priest 2005.]

Prior, A. N. (1971). *Objects of Thought*. Ed. by P. T. Geach and A. J. P. Kenny. Oxford: Clarendon Press.

Quine, W. V. O. (1948/1953). On what there is. In W. V. O. Quine, *From a Logical Point of View: 9 Logico-Philosophical Essays*. Cambridge, MA:

Harvard University Press, 1–19. [Originally published in *The Review of Metaphysics*, 2(5), 1948, 21–38.]

Quine, W. V. O (1969). Existence and quantification. In W. V. O. Quine, *Ontological Relativity and other Essays*. New York: Columbia University Press, 91–113.

Rapaport, W. J. (1978). Meinongian theories and a Russellian paradox. *Noûs*, 12, 153–180.

Rapaport, W. J. (1981). How to make the world fit our language: An essay in Meinongian semantics. *Grazer Philosophische Studien*, 14, 1–21.

Rapaport, W. J. (1985). To be and not to be: Critical study of Terence Parsons's *Nonexistent Objects*. *Noûs*, 19, 255–271.

Reicher, M. E. (2005). Russell, Meinong, and the problem of existent nonexistents. In B. Linsky and G. Imaguire, eds., *On Denoting: 1905–2005*. München: Philosophia, 167–193.

Reicher, M. E. (2006). Two interpretations of "according to a story". In A. Bottani and R. Davies, eds., *Modes of Existence: Papers in Ontology and Philosophical Logic*. Frankfurt am Main: Ontos, 2006, 153–172.

Reicher, M. E. (2008). Review of: *Towards Non-Being. The Logic and Metaphysics of Intentionality*. Oxford: Clarendon Press, 2nd ed. 2007. *Grazer Philosophische Studien*, 76, 255–258.

Reicher, M. E. (2022). Nonexistent objects. In E. N. Zalta, ed., *The Stanford Encyclopedia of Philosophy* (Winter 2022 Edition), https://plato.stanford .edu/entries/nonexistent-objects/.

Rescher, N. (1959). On the logic of existence and denotation. *Philosophical Review*, 68, 157–188.

Rescher, N. (1968). The logic of existence. In N. Rescher, *Topics in Philosophical Logic*. Dordrecht: Reidel, 138–161.

Routley, R. (1979). The semantical structure of fictional discourse. *Poetics*, 8, 3–30.

Routley, R. (1980). *Exploring Meinong's Jungle and Beyond: An Investigation of Noneism and the Theory of Items*, Canberra. [New edition in 4 volumes, each with supplementary essays: M. Eckert, ed., *Exploring Meinong's Jungle and Beyond* (Volume 1, 2018); Dominic Hyde, ed., *Noneist Explorations I* (Volume 2, 2019); Dominic Hyde, ed., *Noneist Explorations II* (Volume 3, 2020); Zach Weber, ed., *Ultralogic as Universal?* (Volume 4, 2019). Cham: Springer.]

Russell, B. (1905a). On denoting. *Mind*, 14(56), 479–493. https://doi.org/ 10.1093/mind/XIV.4.479.

Russell, B. (1905b). Critical notice of *Untersuchungen zur Gegenstandstheorie und Psychologie*, herausgegeben von A. Meinong. *Mind*, 14(56), 530–538.

Russell, B. (1907). Critical notice of *Über die Stellung der Gegenstandstheorie im System der Wissenschaften. Von A. Meinong*. Leipzig: Voigtländer, 1907. Pp. xiii, 159. *Mind*, 16(63), 436–439.

Russell, B. (1910–11). Knowledge by acquaintance and knowledge by description. *Proceedings of the Aristotelian Society*, New Series, 11, 108–128.

Russell, B. (1918–19). The philosophy of logical atomism. [Series of eight lectures, with discussion.] *The Monist*, 28(4), 1918, 495–527 (Lectures I and II), *The Monist*, 29, 1919, 32–63 (Lectures III and IV), 190–222 (Lectures V and VI), and 345–380 (Lectures VII and VIII). [A current edition is in Bertrand Russell, *The Philosophy of Logical Atomism*, with an introduction by D. Pears. London: Routledge, 1985, 1–125.]

Ryle, G. (1933). Symposium: Imaginary objects. *Proceedings of the Aristotelian Society*, Supp. Vol. 12, 18–43.

Ryle, G. (1973). Intentionality-theory and the nature of thinking. *Revue internationale de Philosophie*, 27(2–3), 255–265.

Sainsbury, R. M. (2010). *Fiction and Fictionalism*, London: Routledge.

Salmon, N. (1998). Nonexistence. *Noûs*, 32(3), 277–319.

Schubert Kalsi, M.-L. (1972). *On Emotional Presentation*, Evanston, IL: Northwestern University Press.

Schubert Kalsi, M.-L. (1978). *Alexius Meinong: On Objects of Higher Order and Husserl's Phenomenology*, The Hague: Nijhoff.

Schubert Kalsi, M.-L. (1980). On Meinong's pseudo-objects. *The Southwestern Journal of Philosophy*, 11(1), 115–123.

Sendlak, M. (2022). On the methodological restriction of the principle of characterization. *Erkenntnis*, 87, 807–825.

Simons, P. (1992). On what there isn't: The Meinong-Russell dispute. In P. Simons, *Philosophy and Logic in Central Europe from Bolzano to Tarski. Selected Essays*. Dordrecht: Kluwer, 159–191.

Smith, J. F. (1985). The Russell-Meinong debate. *Philosophy and Phenomenological Research*, 45(3), 305–350.

Smith, J. F. (2005). Russell's "On denoting", the laws of logic and the refutation of Meinong. In B. Linsky and G. Imaguire, eds., *On Denoting: 1905–2005*. München: Philosophia, 137–166.

Strawson, P. F. (1950). On referring. *Mind*, 59(235), 320–344.

Thomasson, A. L. (1999). *Fiction and Metaphysics*, Cambridge: Cambridge University Press.

Thomasson, A. L. (2015). *Ontology Made Easy*, Oxford: Oxford University Press.

van Inwagen, P. (1977). Creatures of fiction. *American Philosophical Quarterly*, 14(4), 299–308.

Voltolini, A. (2006). *How Ficta Follow Fiction. A Syncretistic Account of Fictional Objects*, Dordrecht: Springer.

Walton, K. L. (1990). *Mimesis as Make-Believe: On the Foundations of the Representational Arts*, Cambridge, MA: Harvard University Press.

Wettstein, H. (1984). Did the Greeks really worship Zeus? *Synthese*, 60, 439–450.

Wolterstorff, N. (1980). *Works and Worlds of Art*, Oxford: Clarendon.

Yagisawa, T. (2001). Against creationism in fiction. *Philosophical Perspectives*, 15, 153–172.

Zalta, E. N. (1983). *Abstract Objects: An Introduction to Axiomatic Metaphysics*, Dordrecht: Reidel.

Zalta, E. N. (1988). *Intensional Logic and the Metaphysics of Intentionality*, Cambridge; MA: MIT Press.

Acknowledgments

For numerous helpful critical comments, I am indebted to the series editors Bradley Armour-Garb and Fred Kroon, to two anonymous reviewers, and to Johann Christian Marek. Linguistic advice was provided by Michael Weh. All remaining errors and defects are of course my responsibility.

Cambridge Elements ≡

Philosophy and Logic

Bradley Armour-Garb

SUNY Albany

Bradley Armour-Garb is chair and Professor of Philosophy at SUNY Albany. His books include *The Law of Non-Contradiction* (co-edited with Graham Priest and J. C. Beall, 2004), *Deflationary Truth* and *Deflationism and Paradox* (both co-edited with J. C. Beall, 2005), *Pretense and Pathology* (with James Woodbridge, Cambridge University Press, 2015), *Reflections on the Liar* (2017), and *Fictionalism in Philosophy* (co-edited with Fred Kroon, 2020).

Frederick Kroon

The University of Auckland

Frederick Kroon is Emeritus Professor of Philosophy at the University of Auckland. He has authored numerous papers in formal and philosophical logic, ethics, philosophy of language, and metaphysics, and is the author of *A Critical Introduction to Fictionalism* (with Stuart Brock and Jonathan McKeown-Green, 2018).

About the Series

This Cambridge Elements series provides an extensive overview of the many and varied connections between philosophy and logic. Distinguished authors provide an up-to-date summary of the results of current research in their fields and give their own take on what they believe are the most significant debates influencing research, drawing original conclusions.

Printed in the United States
by Baker & Taylor Publisher Services